Praise for *Mothering by Heart*

"As a mother whose nest is soon to be empty, I appreciated the warmth and wisdom of Cheri's words. Today 'mom' may be your job description, but before you know it, that will change and 'Mom' will become a term of endearment. Take time to be *Mothering by Heart*."

KENDRA SMILEY, Professional Speaker and Author of *High Wire Mom* and *Empowering Choices*, 2001 Illinois Mother of the Year

"This book is a great resource for moms, just like sitting down with a wise and godly woman with her arm around your shoulder sharing her wisdom. Thanks, Cheri, for taking the time to write it all down!"

DENISE GLENN, Founder, MotherWise Ministries

"Pull up a chair, pour yourself a cup of coffee, and get ready to be encouraged. *Mothering by Heart* offers a refreshing, guilt-free, and practical approach to motherhood from God's perspective. Cheri Fuller has done it again. Let her help you relax, rely on God, and actually enjoy being a mom while you're living through those active parenting years. A must read!"

CLAUDIA and DAVID ARP, Authors of *Answering the Eight Cries of the Spirited Child* and *10 Great Dates*

Mothering by
Heart

Mothering by
Heart

Loving Your Kids While Leaning on God

CHERI FULLER

BARBOUR BOOKS
An Imprint of Barbour Publishing, Inc.

The author is represented by and this book is published in association with the literary agency of WordServe Literary Group, Ltd., www.wordserveliterary.com.

Published by Barbour Books, an imprint of Barbour Publishing, Inc., P.O. Box 719, Uhrichsville, Ohio 44683, www.barbourbooks.com

Our mission is to publish and distribute inspirational products offering exceptional value and biblical encouragement to the masses.

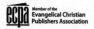

Member of the
Evangelical Christian
Publishers Association

Printed in the United States of America.

In memory of Mama and Mimi

Contents

1

Mothering by Heart

Can you cook. . .that is, besides Macaroni and Cheese from a box?" my aunt asked me one Saturday only a few months before my wedding. It was not a rhetorical question. She knew I'd spent my childhood outside playing instead of in the kitchen learning to cook with Mama.

"Well, no, but just give me some recipes and I can learn!" I replied.

After the wedding, I tucked my trusty wooden recipe box of "no-fail" casserole dishes under my arm, and I was ready to tackle this new challenge with recipes for meaty macaroni, mushroom soup stroganoff, and chili stew. But a few of the recipes weren't as "no-fail" as I'd thought—as I found out one night when the whole house began to have a strange odor after the casserole of the day began to bake. My husband insisted we chuck the entrée, open the windows to air out the duplex, and go out for hamburgers.

Little by little, though, I did learn some cooking skills. I'm not a gourmet cook, but I've managed to feed a family of five.

Many of us approach parenting the way I approached cooking. We're trying to find our way, or perhaps have been parenting a while and have lost our way, so we look for a formula—something concrete and structured that we hope might be the ideal parenting system. But through my years as a mom of children now ages twenty-six, twenty-eight and thirty-one, I've found that the way isn't a formula. Instead, it's connecting with God's heart and with our kids' hearts. As we do, He will lead us and grow us into the moms we're meant to be and the parents our children need.

While there is no one recipe for perfect, foolproof parenting, there's a lot to be gleaned from reading books on child development that give you ideas and suggestions and help you understand the needs of your children as they change and grow. But you should not allow one parenting book or program to overrule your own judgment, silence your own heart response to your child, or leave out how God personally may instruct you concerning your child.

God promises wisdom when you're fresh out of it. He offers hope and comfort when you're discouraged. His joy can give you the strength you need to minister to your family—not just to survive, but to thrive and even enjoy the season you and your children are in. Jesus wants not only to walk alongside you in your mothering journey, but to live through you. And that's one of the main themes of this book—how you can love your kids while you lean on God.

While being a mom is a great privilege and gift, it's also an awesome challenge—and the biggest responsibility you'll ever face! That's why you can't do it in your own strength, but can by depending on the Lord.

Besides fun things like playing at the park with our kids, cheering from the stands in a winning game, cuddling a little one's soft baby face next to yours as you rock him to sleep, or taking photos on birthdays, one of my favorite aspects of mothering is the great spiritual growth potential.

You see, being a mom gives you lots of opportunities to lose your life and to choose your child's good at the expense of your own rights; for example, when it's 2:00 a.m. and your well-deserved sleep is interrupted by a little person who needs you. Or when you'd love to read a magazine, but your children are stir-crazy and want you to read them *Amelia Bedelia* for the fifth time. Or when you see a needed change in your child's life, and as you pray about it, the Lord points out the same need in your life.

So you won't think I'm writing this book because I believe I have "arrived" as a mom, let me share the three prayers most often in my heart when my children were growing up. Since no one except God is a perfect parent, I often prayed, "Lord, please fill the gaps between the love my kids needed today and didn't get from me, even though I was loving them the best I could." My second prayer was, "Jesus, redeem my mistakes." Believe me, I made plenty of them, but I was encouraged that God could use even my blunders to draw my children to Himself. And finally, "Lord, help our marriage, but let it begin in me."

I asked for His mercy and wisdom often because I knew I couldn't do this important job apart from the Lord's grace. That's because just when I got one of my kids figured out and things were in harmony, he or she was off to a new stage with a new set of challenges and reasons for me to be on my knees.

When our oldest child became a teenager I remember my husband and I looking at each other with baffled expressions, saying, "Nothing prepared us for this!" Then after the ups and downs of high school, we adapted to the empty nest. When our kids graduated from college and got married, I faced an entirely new season: being a mother-in-law. (I'm still learning about this one!) Then came a delightful new role as grandma. Maybe these ever-changing seasons of motherhood are God's way of continually drawing us to depend on Him and not on ourselves.

As mothers, we come in different colors, are from unique backgrounds, and live in different parts of the world. But we have a lot in common: We are all working mothers from the minute we leave the delivery room because, as Leslie Parrott said, "[Mothering] depletes, expends, and burns up more time and energy than any other human activity I've encountered. It's a job that never stops. Twenty-four hours a day, seven days a week, a mom is on call to feed, clean, play, and care for her little one."[1] And that's just the first year!

As moms, we want to protect our children. We want the very best for them as we help develop their gifts and talents. We want them to become all they are meant to be! And as Christian mothers, we want our children to know and love Jesus and experience how much He loves them.

In the chapters ahead you won't find ironclad feeding formulas or ways to structure your newborn's schedule so you can get uninterrupted sleep. What you will find addressed are matters of a mother's heart and reflections on becoming the mom you're meant to be—like throwing away the cookie cutter and appreciating each child's individuality; finding a mentor mom to help you along; developing a heart for your home; and not putting off joy so you can really enjoy this brief season of mothering. You'll also discover practical suggestions for making memories, building your child's faith, praying for your child in the midst of a busy life, and moving your body so you'll have enough energy to keep up with your kids and to meet the challenges of each day. You'll find some secrets to effective mothering, such as living out of a sense that people are more important than things, finding words that work to communicate with your kids, and finding creative ways to connect with your children on their turf. Plus there's wisdom from Scripture, from mothers who've gone before you, and a lot of hope, encouragement, and inspiration along the way.

My prayer is that this book will help you find a new joy in whatever season of mothering you're experiencing—because there's so much fun to be had and so much to be enjoyed in the midst of kitchen floors tracked with muddy little footprints and noisy cars full of kids you're carting around. And while each chapter has several suggestions, don't think you have to do it all. Pick one that fits where you are as a mom and try it out, and save the other ideas for a different season. You can ponder the "Question for Reflection" by journaling, praying, or talking it over with a friend at a coffee shop or in a moms' group.

More importantly, as you read, remember: When you get to the end of your rope, you'll find God there. Although I've often found myself fresh out of loving feelings and low on patience, I've found that as Romans 8:36–39 promises, God's love never fails. If you surrender to Him in those "end of your rope, all out of love" moments; receive His love for you; and are willing to be a conduit of His love to your children, husband, and others around you, you'll be amazed at the grace He gives you again and again to be the mom you're meant to be as you love your kids while leaning on God.

2

Throw Away the Cookie Cutter

It was a hot, sunny day, and I was poolside, watching as two neighborhood four-year-olds, Jenny and Olivia, began a swimming lesson.

"Let's play the submarine game and go under the water at the count of three," their instructor, John, said after they had splashed and played around for a few minutes.

Olivia dunked her head and treaded water like a fish, did an underwater handstand, and came up smiling, while her proud mom looked on. But Jenny protested, "I don't like to get my face wet! I don't want to go under!"

"Come on, honey," her mom encouraged from the sidelines. "You can do it. Going under the water is fun."

"No, it's not! I wanna go home," Jenny wailed.

"Okay, we'll play a different game," John suggested. "London Bridge is falling down, falling down, falling down…and when we get to the end of the song, we'll all three go under."

John tried every strategy he knew, but nothing would coax Jenny to join in the submarine or any other game. Normally enthusiastic, she became tearful and anxious, and she didn't enjoy that swimming lesson or the ones that followed. After the first series of lessons was over, her mom wisely gave her a break and just let her play at the pool and go at her own pace. A few weeks later, on her own at the neighborhood pool, she gradually started dipping her face in the water. By the end of the summer, she was having as much fun as the other kids.

> No parent ever trained up his child in the way he should go without making an effort to know that child.
> CHARLES R. SWINDOLL

Why was Olivia so happy to dive in and dunk her head while Jenny resisted? It was not that Olivia's mom did everything right and Jenny's mother didn't. It was about the two girls' unique temperaments. Olivia was a quick-to-warm-up child when faced with a new situation, whereas Jenny was slow to take to anything new—whether it was a new vegetable, a new babysitter, or a new activity, like dunking her head under the water. It also didn't hurt that Olivia's big sister was on the swim team and was a role model for her sister to follow. Jenny, on the other hand, was the oldest and first child in her family to take swimming lessons.

I faced this dilemma when I was a young mother. It seemed all my friends had "easy" babies who were compliant and quick to adjust to new situations. My firstborn, Justin, was determined and strong-spirited. He had a definite mind of his own, even from an early age. While he could be barrels of fun in familiar surroundings, new experiences, like mother-baby swim classes or a switch in preschools, might produce a loud protest.

Was I doing something wrong? I really wanted to be a good mom, to understand my baby, meet his needs and keep my wits about me, but I wasn't sure how to do that.

1. Activity level: Does your child love climbing, running, and large motor playing, or does he prefer less active pastimes like reading and drawing?

2. Predictability and consistency: How predictable or unpredictable are your child's biological functions, like waking and sleeping, feeling hungry, etc.?

3. Response to new situations: What is her first response to new stimuli or unfamiliar situations—a new food, task, person, or classroom? Does she have a negative reaction and act anxious until she's tried it a few times, or jump in enthusiastically?

4. Flexibility and adaptability: Does your child go with the flow and adapt if you're out and her nap has to be later? Or does she thrive on having a set structure to the day?

5. Sensitivity to sudden sounds, textures, and sensory stimuli: Does your child startle easily, awaken to small sounds, cry the minute he's wet, or complain about his clothes irritating his skin? Or does it take more noise and discomfort before he reacts?

6. Positive or negative mood: Some babies wake up after a nap or nighttime sleep in a happy mood while others cry and fuss on awakening. The child who has a more cheerful temperament will likely be the one who sees the cup as "half full" while the fussier child may see the cup as "half empty."

7. High-intensity or low-intensity emotions: Is your

child easygoing about her emotions, or does she protest and cry when frustrated or sad?

8. Easily distracted or highly focused: Does your toddler want to finish his game or block building and become difficult to distract from that goal? Then he's probably a focused rather than easily distracted child.

9. Attention span and persistence level: Does your child have a long attention span and keep persevering when working on a puzzle until it's completed, or does she give up when frustrated?

Fortunately around this time, I found a book written by two wise child psychiatrists, Drs. Stella Chess and Alexander Thomas, called *Know Your Child*. When I saw the title on the bookshelf, I thought, "That's just what I need! I want to know and understand my child." In the book, Chess and Thomas report findings from their twenty-five-year study of people from infancy to adulthood. From birth onward, they explain, individuals vary in their behavior and their reactions to different life experiences. These variations indicate specific temperamental differences. In each category, the authors rate individuals as mild or intense, high or low, quick or slow.

One of the most important things I discovered in this book was the term "goodness of fit" or "attunement." More important than children having "ideal" characteristics—such as adaptability and compliance—that make them easy to deal with, is the "fit" that grows between parent and child. For example, what demands and expectations do I have for my child? What reactions does my child's behavior create in me? And what reactions does my behavior create in him? Do I accept, enjoy, and delight in my child, or am I continually frustrated or disappointed with his behavior?

> As parents affirm each child's uniqueness, the children will find it easier to believe that God accepts them just as they are.

NORM WRIGHT

A few years later, I learned about children's different intelligence types and learning styles, which refers to the ways of processing the information they need to learn. These concepts were a godsend for me. It helped me better understand, accept, and enjoy the wonderful gift of our firstborn son, then a few years later, his brother and sister. I began to realize that some of the things we were experiencing were more about differences in temperament between him and me or between him and my friends' kids. He was merely responding to experiences from his unique temperament and personality or, you might say, the way God had wired him.

The more I understood about our little one's emotional makeup, the more accepting I was of his emotions and the more grateful I became for his individuality—and in fact, able to celebrate his wonderful and lively personality. I was more patient with his spirited behavior. Because he was determined and persistent, I realized I needed to major on the majors, instead of the minors, in discipline issues—which means being firm on a few issues instead of enforcing many rules and saying no all the time.

> *For you formed my inward parts; you knitted me together in my mother's womb. I praise you, for I am fearfully and*

wonderfully made. Wonderful are your works; my soul knows it very well.

PSALM 139:13–14 ESV

When I stopped comparing him to the "compliant kids," I began to find ways to encourage his gifts and strengths. I saw his energy and persistence as traits that would be helpful when he faced challenges. (And truly, they are some of the strengths that contribute to the marvelous, successful adult he is today.) As I embraced his uniqueness, the "goodness of fit" between my son and me grew into a wonderful relationship that has lasted.

Our second child, Chris, was completely different—of course! And Alison, number three, was a whole new challenge and joy. Each of them has a distinct temperament, learning style, and set of gifts. Justin's learning strength is auditory, Chris's more visual, and Alison's kinesthetic and visual. They each have different intelligence strengths and talents, too—my oldest son: communication, teaching, leadership, and people skills; my younger son: analytical, spatial, musical, and artistic talent; and my daughter: musical, language, art, and creative gifts. Each one is precious in his or her own way, fearfully and wonderfully made by our Creator, but definitely unique!

I figure God doesn't want us to rest on our laurels. Just when we've figured out one of our kids, He gives us another that baffles us completely. I think it's His way of keeping us on our toes (and knees). And besides, think how boring it would be if each of your children had the same temperament, interests, and gifts. Here are some ways to throw away the cookie-cutter approach and get a handle on your child's uniqueness. As you review the lists with their clues to temperament, learning style, and intelligence type, consider the suggestions below them. Keep in mind, this isn't a labeling exercise or a one-pronged approach to understanding your child. But looking at the characteristics will help you gain a big picture of your child's individuality.

LEARNING STYLE

Imagine you're reading aloud from a book with the repeated refrain "and the rabbit went hop, hop, hop." Does your child:

- Come up close, perhaps insisting on being on your lap, to see the pictures? This is a sign of a visual learner.
- Mimic the words of the refrain or interrupt to talk about the story? This is a sign of an auditory learner.
- Move around and do what the refrain says—hop, hop, hop? This is a sign of a kinesthetic learner.

"I wish he were organized like his big sister." "I wish she made high grades like Mary's daughter." "I wish the twins were athletic like the rest of the family." As John Drescher says, "Continual comparison builds inferiority feelings which harm personality development."[3] Comparison also causes kids to feel unaccepted for who they are. Instead of comparing, recognize and celebrate each of your kids' different God-given abilities, gifts, and personalities.

Look for the silver lining. Be aware that often what looks like a negative trait in childhood can become a terrific strength in adulthood. For example, argumentative kids usually possess an analytical talent that can help them become a successful scientist, doctor, or engineer. Bossiness in childhood is a key marker for leadership, which means your bossy child may be the future CEO of a corporation. The emotional or melancholy child can develop into an artist or actor. As an adult, the very active kid who ran his mom ragged has great energy for tasks and challenges.

DIFFERENT KINDS OF SMART

- **The Musical Child** is always singing a song (usually, right on pitch) or moving to a beat. He easily remembers tone, rhythm, and melody.
- **The People Smart Child** is a social butterfly, loves to be with a group playing and taking the lead, and has great communication skills.
- **The Body Smart Child** has extra energy and loves sports. She remembers songs with body movements the best.
- **The Spatially Smart Child** can look at directions in an interlocking block set and put the whole project together. He enjoys drawing, solving puzzles and mazes, and designing things.
- **The Math Smart Child** is always sorting, classifying, sequencing objects, and analyzing things.
- **The Verbally Smart Child** loves word play, telling stories, and listening to books being read. She has an uncanny memory for words.

(Based on concepts in Dr. Howard Gardner's book *Frames of Mind: The Theory of Multiple Intelligence*)

Watch, look, and listen, when your kids are playing, reading, studying, interacting with others. Turn the TV, laptop, and smartphone off and tune in to your child on a regular basis. Then pray for a spirit of wisdom, understanding, and revelation (see Colossians 1:9–12) to see your children's hearts and personalities from God's perspective, to discover what motivates them and to know how best to nurture and guide them.

QUESTION FOR REFLECTION

What do you love most about each of your children, and what do you find most frustrating? From the lists you've written, what are some unique things about each of your kids? Thank God for all of these things.

3

Don't Put off Joy

"When my little girl gets potty trained, then it's all going to smooth out," said a mother of preschoolers. "When I lose the extra twenty-five pounds I gained in pregnancy, I'm going to be so much happier," said the young mom sitting next to me at a luncheon I spoke at.

"When my son starts school on a full-day basis, then finally I'll get something done. With half-day kindergarten, I just get him dropped off and it's time to go pick him up. He's a bit difficult at this stage and, frankly, I'm exhausted," said another young woman at our table. "I can't wait for him to grow out of this stage!"

If you're like these moms and so many others, you often find yourself thinking that you'll experience joy when. . .

- the finances aren't so tight and you have more money in your checking account;
- your prodigal teen turns around, starts loving God and isn't attracted to the wild kids, and makes better grades and choices;
- your baby's teeth come in so she's not so fussy and starts sleeping all night, letting you get some much-needed rest.

The list of "whens and ifs" is endless, and these are all good goals. But if you stake your joy on "whens and ifs," you will find yourself perpetually frustrated, missing out on the joys and blessings God has for you in each season of life, even those that are difficult and filled with unfinished projects, teething babies, toddlers resisting potty training, or challenging teens.

One thing for sure, the season you are in now—whether pregnancy, caring for babies or preschoolers, or parenting teens—will soon be gone.

Throughout Scripture, God reminds us that life is short, and we can't count on what will happen tomorrow. For example, James 4:14 says, "Why, you do not even know what will happen tomorrow. What is your life? You are a mist that appears for a little while and then vanishes." Psalm 90:10 says, "For [the years] quickly pass, and we fly away."

> *This is the day that the LORD has made; let us rejoice and be glad in it.*
>
> PSALM 118:24 ESV

We can't make our years go any more slowly or control circumstances (such as the baby's teeth coming in or our teenager's heart finally turning back to God). But we can choose our attitude and find that there's a lot of joy to be had right where we are if we look for it.

Here are some ways to not put off joy:

Make room for fun and for things you and your kids really enjoy. I think parenthood is a great excuse to go to the park, ride bikes, and play baseball like you did when you were young. What's fun for your family might be going to the zoo or having a picnic. Maybe you enjoy going to the library for story times and puppet shows. Even if it's rainy, you can invite another mother and her children over for lunch and let your kids help you make a special treat— like "Ants on a Log" (raisins on a celery stick spread with peanut butter) or "Happy Face Pear Salad" (half a canned pear with a dot of mayonnaise and raisins to make a happy face).

Take advantage of seasonal joys. There is something in every season to enjoy: picking strawberries and camping out in the backyard in summer, visiting a local pumpkin patch for that perfect pumpkin in the fall, baking gingerbread cookies and drinking hot chocolate in the winter. In the spring, when smells and colors seem more vivid after the long winter, take "smelly walks" with your kids. Just stroll around the block and have them name all the things they can smell. For a "color walk," choose a color for the day—for instance, red—and during your walk, have the kids point out all the red things they see.

> There is not one blade of grass, there is no color in this world that is not intended to make us rejoice.
>
> JOHN CALVIN

Find joy. . .even when your kids are sick. From time to time, when your children are sick and stuck inside, you've probably felt that a dark cloud has drifted over your home. That cloud used to drift over our home when our oldest had asthma attacks or when all three children were sick at the same time with strep throat— that is, until I began to see sick days as a time to fill up my kids' emotional tanks with TLC, a time to hug, fix hot apple juice, and read books together aloud. Instead of thinking everything will be better when your children are well, try making the most of their downtime.

Every day, there are miracles and things to celebrate: a purple-and-red sunset, an e-mail from an old friend, your child's first sentence, a sticky kiss, or even a goldfinch or cardinal at your bird feeder.

> Every day brings a chance for you to draw in a breath,
> kick off your shoes, and dance.
>
> Unknown

But the best way to experience the greatest joy is just to. . .

Give yourself away. An old saying goes: "The joy that you give to others is the joy that comes back to you." When we are concerned about others and how we can be a blessing to them today, when we are being God's hands and expressing His love to others, He fills us with an unquenchable joy.

Question for Reflection

What are some everyday miracles you've experienced lately? What are three things you really gain a lot of joy from doing? (Pick one and make time to do it this week.)

4

People Are More Important Than Things

Lisa, a young mother of two, set her sights on transforming an antique, six-by-four-foot farmhouse table that had been in the family for years. It would mean stripping the piece of its seven layers of paint, restaining it, and putting on several coats of polyurethane. But she was ready for the task.

With Grandma helping with the kids, Lisa began Monday morning and got as far as stripping the top when other duties called her away. All day Tuesday was spent working with a loud power stripper, and by the end of the day, her muscles were shaking with fatigue. Wednesday she labored in 104-degree heat in the garage, sanding and staining the table.

Early Thursday morning, Lisa applied the first coat of polyurethane. Friday she put on coats number two and three. On Saturday she got out to the garage early because she could hardly wait to put the final coat of polyurethane on this absolutely gorgeous table. A friend who dropped by told Lisa her handiwork was stunning; the tabletop looked like it had glass on it because she could see her reflection. For fifteen minutes, Lisa basked in the glow of that comment and just stood back and admired all she'd accomplished that week. She couldn't wait for the table to be sitting in her kitchen in a few days, her family enjoying a meal on it.

When another friend dropped by and told her how beautiful the table was, Lisa was busy cleaning up rags and brushes. As she was talking with her friend, she heard, "Look, Mommy, I can help you!"

Her little Samantha, four years old, had gone into the storage room, picked up the paintbrush that had been soaking in gasoline, and was sloshing it enthusiastically across the top of that perfectly smooth table. "See how I'm helping you with the table, Mommy!"

Lisa felt every muscle in her body go limp. She froze in shock. The only words that would come out of her mouth were "Ohhhh, noooooo!" All those hours of work in the heat. All that stripping, sanding, painting—all ruined. She wanted to yell, "Samantha, how could you do this? You know how hard Mommy has worked on this! Why did you do it?" But she held the words back and took a deep breath.

> *But we were gentle among you, like a nursing mother taking care of her own children.*
>
> 1 THESSALONIANS 2:7 ESV

Samantha's smile turned into a very sad expression as she suddenly realized she wasn't really helping her mommy. Lisa tried to explain that the brush didn't have paint on it but a chemical that eats through paint. She assured her daughter, "It's going to be okay, honey. Let me think for a minute. Why don't you go to your room and I'll come up soon." This exhausted mom needed a few minutes alone to calm down and think.

Later when they talked, Lisa told Samantha that she could

fix the table and they'd love it no matter how it turned out. Lisa called her dad, and he told her what to do to redeem the table. But it took four more long, hot days of working to undo the damage and repair the finish.

The table now sits in Lisa's kitchen with burn marks from the stripper. (Using it twice burned the table's surface in places.) Its flaws are a constant reminder to Lisa that people are more important than things.

Is the table as perfect as the first time she refinished it? No. But is it really that important? No. Lisa knows it is just a table and her daughter is a wonderful creation of God, with a radiance and light in her that truly is like glass. You can see through her a reflection of Jesus. . .now that is what truly matters.

Lisa could have wounded Samantha's spirit that day if she'd been more concerned about the less-than-perfect table than her daughter's heart. But long before this mishap, she'd made the decision that people are more important than things, and that included antique tables.

> A sparkling house is a fine thing if the children aren't
> robbed of their luster in keeping it that way.
>
> MARCELENE COX

Our culture encourages us to value money, possessions, a picture-perfect house, and gourmet meals above spending time with our kids. But when you focus on keeping a perfect house, keeping up appearances, and making everything look "right" (including the kids), your perspective gets skewed.

God sometimes brings an unlikely person into your life to

help you rearrange your priorities. One day, a woman I know was delivering something to her friend Karen. When she knocked on the door, there was no answer, so she just went into the house. She lived in a small town where people felt safe leaving their doors unlocked. When she entered, she saw piles of laundry, unwashed dishes, and a general mess. Her first thought was, "Why isn't Karen here taking care of things? My house is sparkling at all times."

> Remember what counts. Little things and little people
> weigh heavily in the scales of heaven. Remember what it
> was like to be this size when wonder came so easily.
> Remember how it felt to always be looking up.
> DEENA LEE WILSON

When she looked out into the backyard, she saw Karen with her five small children gathered around her in a tight circle. They were very excited about what they were doing. She went out and discovered that Karen and her kids were watching a trail of ants. That day changed this woman's mind forever about her priorities, because she realized that if Karen had been inside doing the laundry and cleaning the house, she and her children would have missed the ants.

QUESTION FOR REFLECTION

What's most important to you? Is there a "trail of ants" your kids are missing out on today because you are too busy keeping a perfect home?

5

Follow the Leader

Jordan put her hands on her hips, pointed her finger, and said, "You will just have to go to time out!" She was reprimanding her mom, who had lost her temper when the dog got out, making her chase him around the neighborhood. Kathy laughed as she realized how much her daughter sounded just like she did.

Most of us have seen our children do mirror-image imitations of things we've said or done. As a wise older mom once told me, "Kids seldom misquote you. They more often repeat word for word what you shouldn't have said."

But the good news is that the very way our kids watch us and imitate what we do can be a powerful tool for motivating them in positive ways.

"I want my kids to be motivated. I want them to like learning, not to look at it as drudgery!" say countless moms in groups I've spoken to. In fact, you have within you the best motivator of all—your position as a role model.

"Actions speak louder than words," my dad always said, and he was right. Words are important, but actions impact our children even more and are more often imitated by them. Like it or not, kids play "Follow the Leader," and for many years we—as moms and dads—are the leaders. Our children mirror our attitudes and habits in so many areas.

The dictionary defines *model* as "a person or thing which is regarded as a standard of excellence to be imitated." You and I may not feel like a standard of excellence, but kids are careful observers of what we do. Watching adults is the primary way kids learn about acceptable attitudes and behaviors. Whatever they see us do, they assume is okay for them to do too—whether that's telling the truth, overusing smartphones at the expense of being present with people, or being kind to others. They internalize what we do as the values they will live by.

Studies about the use of seat belts, tobacco, alcohol, and drugs show that the main factor determining whether kids say yes or no is their parents' example.

For instance, one survey showed that mothers have the greatest influence on getting children to wear seat belts in cars. More than TV or school campaigns featuring sports heroes, movie stars, or police officers, seeing Mom buckle up has a powerful effect on kids' safety habits. The same principle holds true for smoking, eating, television viewing, drinking, table manners, and language habits—children tend to do what their parents do, not what they say.

> Children are born mimics. They behave like their parents
> despite all our efforts to tell them how to act properly.
>
> UNKNOWN

Don't get me wrong, dad also has a big impact on the kids' desire to learn and achieve, but mom is usually the point person when it comes to school involvement, helping with homework, and learning. And mothers tend to spend the most time with the kids. This is both a happy and a scary thought—such a big responsibility we moms have!

But let's think about it positively for a moment and how being a positive role model can help your children become motivated learners. Motivation happens to kids with parents who are intellectually alive and show excitement over the world of books, ideas, and numbers—it's contagious, say experts.

A child will catch a love of learning from a mom who likes to find things out, who is curious herself, who enjoys learning for its own sake, who adds to her store of knowledge simply because it's fun. It's not that hard, either, to be a good example in this way. Try these suggestions:

Keep learning. If you don't know something—like how to grow cactus or make grapevine wreaths, for example—head for the library with your child. Let him see you check out the computerized card catalog, ask the library staff for help, and find the resources. If you take a workshop at a hobby store or local community college, your actions motivate your child to dig for useful information on things that interest him. Besides, learning something new keeps our brains sharp, which we need if we're going to keep up with our kids as they grow.

One mother can achieve more than a hundred teachers.

JEWISH PROVERB

Model writing and reading. When you write a letter to a great-aunt who's not on the Internet, when you pen a thank-you note, or type a letter of complaint to a business, let your kids see what you're doing. They will understand the usefulness of writing. If you're an avid reader and spend more time reading than watching TV, if your kids hear you laugh as you read the Sunday comics or find you enjoying a good novel, then they are more likely to catch the magic of reading. And if they see you reading the Bible and spending time with God as a regular part of your day, then they'll know how important God and His Word are. Your actions can be the best sermon of all.

Admit your mistakes. Even in our mistakes, we can be good role models! When you're willing to admit your errors, learn from your failures, and ask forgiveness when you hurt someone, then kids learn the value of repentance and how to handle mistakes—because we all make them! They tend to risk making mistakes in order to grow, knowing they have the support of parents who aren't perfect—just forgiven.

QUESTION FOR REFLECTION

What are some positive examples you can set for your children this week to build up their character or boost their motivation?

6

Teaching Your Kids to Pray

Patty, a young woman I know, was just finishing helping her boys' with their schoolwork for the day when the telephone rang.

"The trees near our home are on fire!" her sister Marianne yelled. "The fire department is already here. They told us to get any important paperwork and medications and get out. We only have ten minutes until the flames reach our house!" Marianne's family lived on several acres of land surrounded by dense woods, and the drought in Texas only made the fire spread more quickly.

As Marianne grabbed photo albums and ripped pictures off the walls, she pleaded, "Pray for us!"

Patty promised she would and shot an arrow prayer for God's protection of her sister's home and family as she opened the cabinet door to get the prayer chain phone numbers. I'll get all the prayers I know mobilized, she thought as she dialed the first number. As she hung up the phone to call another, Patty realized her second grader, Andrew, and his older brother, Grant, had overheard the conversation. She knew then that the chain of prayer needed to begin right there with her boys.

Patty ran for her Bible and, holding hands with Grant and Andrew, prayed with them that God would hold the fire back from her sister's house, save as many trees and as much land as possible, and give the firemen the advantage over the flames. Then she suggested Grant read Psalm 91 aloud to Andrew and pray with him while she contacted others on the prayer chain.

While making the rest of the calls, Patty could see her boys in the next room on their knees interceding for their cousins, aunt, and uncle. When their mom rejoined them, they continued praying Psalm 91 and lingered on verses 9 and 10, which say, "If you say, 'the LORD is my refuge,' and you make the Most High your dwelling, no harm will overtake you, no disaster will come near your tent." Remembering that Marianne had named her house "Crosswings" several years before, they prayed verse 4, asking that God would cover the home with His feathers and that the family would find refuge under His wings as the angels held back the flames.

Minutes flew by as they prayed and read the verses, and before long, the phone rang again. Patty leaped to answer it, her heart racing. It was Marianne again, but this time with good news. The fire had burned eight acres and come as close as thirty-seven footsteps from their house when it was stopped. Firefighters were still working on the embers, but the blaze was under control and their home was saved.

All your children shall be taught by the LORD, and great shall be the peace of your children.

ISAIAH 54:13 NKJV

Patty was so glad she'd brought her boys into the circle of prayer and that they had the hands-on opportunity to go into action instead of worrying and feeling helpless when something bad happened. She was even happier that they had seen God's mighty response.

But it doesn't take a crisis to find reasons to pray with your children. There are plenty of everyday problems, situations, family needs, and concerns of others to pray about together. And when prayer is your first response instead of a last resort, you help your kids learn the value of going to God with the little things as well as the big ones.

When I speak on prayer, moms often ask me, "How can I teach my children to pray?" Here are some ways:

Be a pray-er yourself, and ask your kids to partner with you in prayer. Just like chicken pox or the common cold, the motivation to pray is contagious. Kids catch it from parents who talk and listen to God with their children in the spontaneous moments of living together. The most powerful teaching tool you have is to respond with the power of prayer to all the needs, burdens, concerns, and problems you face.

> Prayer is as simple as a child making known its wants to its parents.
>
> UNKNOWN

Help your kids see things around them as visual aids to prompt prayer. When they see a parking spot for disabled people, they could pray for those with special needs and disabilities. If you're driving and hear a siren or see an ambulance speeding down the street, ask one of your kids to send a prayer heavenward for the emergency room workers who will treat the injured people and for safety for the ambulance drivers. And just as Patty did, bring your kids into the prayer circle when there is a problem or emergency situation you see or hear about.

Pray conversationally. Instead of saying a rote prayer over meals or formalizing prayer, speak to God as a friend. Use simple, conversational language and short sentences rather than long, flowery, formal words. Then kids will think, "I can do that" and are more apt to talk to God in their own way and know that He hears them. Encourage your children that short petitions, like "Help, God" or "Thank You, Lord," are wonderful prayers. And give them a hands-on way to pray, like putting a globe in the middle of the dinner table and having each person spin it and pray a short prayer of blessing or whatever comes to mind for the country their hands land on.

Ground your prayers in God's Word. Have your kids ever said, "I don't know what to say!" when you ask them to pray? Teach them how the Bible can shape their prayers. When kids learn to pray God's Word, their prayer vocabulary increases, and they grow in confidence because their prayers hit the target and are right in line with God's best for their lives. Praying verses like Philippians 4:13: "Lord, thank You that I can do all things (even my hard math homework) because You give me strength" or Psalm 106:1: "Thank You, Lord! How good You are!" can jump-start their conversation with God.

> A prayer prayed from the heart of the child to the Father is never in vain.
>
> ELISABETH ELLIOT

As you take the ordinary experiences of life and turn them into prayer moments with your kids, you'll be guiding them into a closer relationship with their heavenly Father, and they will discover an invaluable source of help and grace for the rest of their lives.

QUESTION FOR REFLECTION

What is your family's greatest need? Look for a scripture that addresses that need and pray it together.

7

A Heart for Your Home

In these days of fast-forward living and ever-changing mobility, it is easy for the place you live to become a pit stop—a place to drop in and microwave something to eat or change clothes between activities, but not a home where real life happens. Sometimes we have a sense that what's happening "out there," at that place we're rushing to get to, is much more important than what's going on inside our own four walls. Then there's the whole matter of how you create a home. And if you're living "temporary," that's a challenge. But even in a duplex or tiny apartment, you can bring your heart—your personality, uniqueness, and creativity—to create a home.

When Holmes and I married in 1969, we lived in a one-bedroom duplex in a little old neighborhood in Waco, Texas. We had a very small budget: $27 a week for groceries, $115 for rent, $5 a week for gas, and little for new furniture or accessories. We had a Kmart wicker settee with an orange corduroy cushion from my parents, a lovely set of dishes that were wedding presents, some kitchen stuff, and a little box full of recipes I couldn't wait to try out. Fortunately, the place came with a bed, a dresser, and an old dining-room table because we didn't have those items.

We put our candlesticks (a wedding present) on the table, and Holmes made a lamp for the living room. After a few months, we saved enough to go to the flea market where we found an old architect's table for $10 to put plants on and a few used frames for inexpensive art prints we had gotten at a museum gift shop.

It wouldn't make the Pottery Barn catalog, but it was home! I graded papers there at night since I taught English by day. We had friends over for spaghetti or ice cream. It was just temporary—we only lived there a year and a half. After four houses in the neighborhood were robbed, we found another little house to rent.

Anyone can build a house. We need the Lord for the creation of a home.

JOHN HENRY JOWETT

In each place we lived, we painted, fixed up, sewed curtains (that was my job), and put up wallpaper—creating a place to call home. When the kids came along, we refurbished a rocking chair, made a Raggedy Andy wall decoration, and painted an unfinished little dresser with bright lime green, blue, and yellow drawers (remember, it was the 1970s). We thought we'd created the cutest nursery ever! How can you build a home, a place where your own and your family's hearts are rejuvenated, where creativity takes place, memories are made, books are read, and laughter and games are mixed in with the chores?

Surround yourself with stuff you and your spouse love, things that have meaning and depth to you, such as a treasured collection of stories, items from your favorite hobby, flowers (home-grown if you can't afford the florist's variety), family photos, a collection of shells or something else special to you, or a quilt to wrap up in when you're cold.

Paint and fix up now, not later. Don't wait until you're putting your house on the market to hang wallpaper, paint, or complete those projects that would make it more livable and comfortable. And don't wait until the decor is "perfect" or until you have a bigger dining room or a new table and chairs to ask friends over for dinner. Fresh paint, homemade curtains, and photos hung on a special wall can help make a place more inviting. Do these things soon after moving in so you can really enjoy where you live right from the start, for as long as you're there. Remember, all our houses on earth are temporary, even if we own them. Our real Dwelling Place is the Lord, and when we get to heaven, we won't ever have to pack again!

> Home is not just a place you live—it's a place you grow.
> CHRISTINA, AGE 8

Pray for a heart for your home. Once you have the walls painted and furniture arranged, it is easy to become so focused on your job, church, grad school, or other activities that you neglect your home and have little left to give your family. Creating a home—with a semblance of order, loveliness, warm hospitality, and cherished memories—takes the heart of someone who wants to make a home. If your heart needs some warming toward home, ask God for that desire. Ask Him for whatever is lacking—a sense of order, a bigger picture of your influence, or a mentor who can share practical tips and help you along in the area of homemaking.

Overwhelmed by the piles? As a young mother, I was secretly always hoping my fairy godmother would show up, zip around like Mr. Clean, and shine up my house, especially on days when I was tired and overwhelmed by mounds of laundry and dirty dishes. I was not a natural organizer! Lisabeth, a woman who invited us younger moms from the church to her house for a "Prayer and Share" group, had the most amazingly organized house, and I loved just peeking in her perfectly arranged drawers and cabinets. Being with her (and asking her questions) inspired me and caused me to ask God even more—Lord, help me in this area of homemaking!

And you know what? He did. My sweet husband also often came alongside me, pitching in and helping out. We found that what worked for us as a family (especially when I was teaching part-time and helping Holmes at his store) was doing two hours of chores on Saturday, all together. It was a team approach. Everybody had a list, including the kids, and afterward, we went out to the park or for pizza. Find what works for you.

Simple Things that Make a Home a Refuge

- Play CDs of soothing classical or Christian music, or turn on the classical radio station as a background rather than the TV.
- Start dinner earlier in the day by making a casserole. Later, add store-bought french bread (or made-in-your-oven bread) and salad in a bag, and voilà!—a lovely meal for you and your family or even a guest. Then during the pre-dinner hour, when kids are often the crankiest, anxious for dad to come home, make it a "happy hour." Put out fresh veggies and dip, or fruit slices with cheese, and play a game.
- Ask for God's love and peace to fill your heart and home each day.

What makes you feel at home? A nook for your hobby, a throw to cuddle up in for an impromptu nap, a few green plants, a basket of books? What would it take for you to "build" your home?

Ah! There is nothing like staying at home, for real comfort.

JANE AUSTEN

8

Fingerprints on the Wall

I raced into the grocery store, eight-month-old in my arms and three-year-old in hand, to pick up Tylenol, a prescription, apple juice, and a few other groceries. I was on my way home from the doctor's office, and my "To Do" list was nowhere near done. There was dinner to cook, as well as housework and a Master's thesis I was working on that awaited me at home.

I gathered up the things I needed and hit the checkout counter, impatiently waiting to get my change so I could dash out the door, when all of a sudden, an older woman came up behind me in the line. She stopped me and said, "Slow down and enjoy your boys while they're little. The time will go so fast! My two sons are now grown and live on different coasts. How I miss them and wish I could spend the day with them!"

The time didn't seem to be going fast. In fact, some days it seemed to be crawling. Those were the days when I could barely see over the stacks of dirty diapers, when I was cooped up with my children's bouts of bronchitis or ear infections, spilled milk, and whines of "Mommy!" On those days, it seemed like I hadn't talked to an adult in weeks. It didn't help that Holmes worked long hours and, since we were newcomers to the city, I didn't know any other moms.

Yet I knew the woman was right. And when I went home that

day, I slowed down enough to make block forts and castles with my boys then stroll them to the park to play.

Perhaps you've received similar advice from an older mom, too—but it bears pondering again. Because the truth is, your kids' childhood will pass so quickly. You know they'll grow up someday. But in reality, that day comes so soon. In the twinkling of an eye, each of your kids will be taking off for college or career. Try this little exercise: Close your eyes and picture your child strolling down the aisle with his graduating class. Decked out in cap and gown, he walks across the stage when his name is called and grasps his diploma. Then a few short months later, he piles all his stuff in his car and heads across the country for college. When that happens, you won't be thinking, "I wish I'd spent more time at the office or polishing the floors."

> It will be gone before you know it. The fingerprints
> on the wall will appear higher and higher, and then
> suddenly they disappear.
>
> DOROTHY EVSLIN

I remember the morning after our oldest son Justin got married. I was getting dressed when all of a sudden, I thought I heard his distinctive, wonderful laugh coming from the front of the house. Oh, how I loved that laugh. But then with a feeling of sadness, I thought, "No, that can't be Justin. He doesn't live here anymore. He has his own place where he and Tiffany will live." Besides, I knew they were on their honeymoon. But in that moment, the house seemed very quiet. Graduation photos on the piano. Toys stored in the attic. No music blaring from his room.

Perhaps your home is still filled with the footsteps of little (or big) kids that run, skip, or jump but rarely walk. Lucky you! Or you're on the verge of seeing your kids fly from the nest. Like my friend Melina told me one summer, "In two years Gib will be gone to college! I wish I could make time stop! It is moving too fast!"

You can't make time stop as life proceeds and your children grow, so what can you do to savor and enjoy the time you do have together? How can a mother make the most of those fleeting, sometimes exhausting, yet sweet years of child rearing?

> Perhaps parents would enjoy their children more if they stopped to realize the film of childhood can never be run through for a second showing.
>
> EVELYN NOWN

See your life in seasons. Recognize that as women, our lives change in a seasonal way and that no family situation is static. Lives and possibilities will be different five or ten years down the road. Recognizing this truth is especially vital today because we have a tendency to think we have to do everything this year or achieve certain goals before age thirty. It is also an important truth to consider when making decisions about work and finances that will impact the family.

As Brenda Hunter said, there is "world enough and time" to dream new dreams, pursue careers, and focus energies in different directions after children are raised. "We can have it all—but not all at once," she says. "And if we live each day fully, we won't look back over the terrain of our lives with emotional pain because we were inaccessible to our families while our children were at home."[4]

I met a woman recently on a plane who had raised five children as a stay-at-home mom. Afterward, she earned one master's degree in criminal justice, worked with juveniles who were in trouble with the law, and went on to earn another master's degree in psychology. When I met her, she had practiced as a marriage and family counselor for over ten years and was more energetic than most thirty-year-olds. She was pursuing goals she wanted to fulfill and was still going strong in her 60s.

> There is so little empty space. The space is scribbled on,
> the time has been filled. Too many activities, and people,
> and things. . . For it is not merely the trivial which
> clutters our lives but the important as well.
> ANNE MORROW LINDBERGH

Even while you're in your active parenting years, you can develop your gifts and talents. You can volunteer in your child's school, homeschool co-op group, church, or community. There are also home businesses, flextime jobs, and other options that help a mom keep family as a priority. If you love painting, set up a corner of a room to paint. If gardening is your passion, let the yard be your canvas. If you love writing or any other creative pursuit, schedule blocks of time to pursue your craft.

Find your own "slow-down spots of time" together. "Slow down is my best advice to young mothers," said Leonette, an older woman I once met. "We can get so involved with doing things and getting everything done that we begin to look at our children as interruptions instead of priorities," she added. Lying on a quilt looking up at the night sky's constellations, you will find that time slows down a little. Moments sitting on the edge of your child's bed to listen, encourage, and pray for her concerns are precious. So is taking time for a walk, sharing an ice cream sundae, or reading in sleeping bags by the fireplace.

> *So teach us to number our days that we may get a heart of wisdom.*
>
> PSALM 90:12 ESV

Don't let yourself and your kids get so busy and overcommitted that you're constantly rushing from one place to another. A recent study showed that the main cause of tension in women's lives is too much to do and not enough time to do it, feeling like splintered fragments, going in too many directions. Instead of overscheduling your and your children's days so that there's no lag time at all, try letting each child pick one extracurricular activity every six months just for themselves and one activity during each week you do together as a family.

Life is a gift. Every day is a gift. As you give your time to God each morning, keep in mind what's most important. Then like the girl who spun straw into gold in the fairy tale "Rumpelstiltskin," you can use this time and see each moment turn into gold.

QUESTION FOR REFLECTION

What really matters to you? Write down what are the most important, non-negotiable things in your life. They could include: The love of spouse, kids, family, and friends. The joy of knowing

God. Helping a friend who has just lost her child or is in the hospital. Time to take a walk, create something, or sing a song. Making your house a place of hospitality. Teaching your kids and helping them know Jesus. Then ask yourself, Am I using my time to do these things and attain these goals?

9
A Mom Who Listens

A mom I met at a conference shared with me about a time she was bustling in the kitchen, fixing dinner for company. Her little boy, Matt, was following her around, pulling on her skirt, trying to tell her what had happened that day at school.

"Mommy, I was on the playground and Jake ran up and hit me and I fell out of the swing and I didn't know what to do, so I. . ."

"Oh, honey, I've got to get dinner fixed, and I'm way behind," she replied.

"Here's the picture I colored. Look!" Matt said.

"In a few minutes, when I finish this I can look at it."

He kept on talking, telling her another story. As he was wrapping it up he asked, "Are you listening, Mommy?"

"Sure, honey," his mom said as she turned off the mixer and started setting the table.

Finally, Matt stopped her. She stooped down, and they looked at each other eye to eye. He put his little hands on her cheeks and said, "But Mommy, would you listen with your face?"

Many of us are like that mother. Talking we can handle. Listening, especially with our full attention, is more challenging. Sometimes we're too busy to listen or too distracted or feeding the baby or on the computer or juggling multiple tasks.

But before long, we wonder why our kids won't talk to us

(especially when they get to the preteen and teen years) and wish they would. What we've forgotten is that 80 percent of the communication process is listening.

Somebody once said that the fact God gave us two ears and one mouth should give us a clue. But while listening is the most important aspect of communication, it is often the most neglected.

Take a moment to listen today.
To what your children are trying to say. . .
Listen to their problems,
Listen for their needs. . .
Tolerate their chatter,
Amplify their laughter,
Find out what's the matter,
Find out what they're after,
But tell them that you love them every single night. . .
Listen today, whatever you do,
And they will come back to listen to you.
UNKNOWN

Becoming a better listener has been a long journey for me. I came from a family of five girls, all talkers, and a little brother who had to work hard to get a word in edgewise but who managed! When I realized how deficient I was in this area—I made listening one of my goals. I haven't arrived, but I have discovered some ways to improve:

Look close. When your child is talking, give her eye contact and pay attention to her words, feelings, and body language.

Start small. Instead of aiming to listen to your child for an hour or two, start with a goal of spending five or ten minutes a day listening to her, perhaps while you're chopping vegetables, playing a board game, or throwing a ball outside.

Be available to talk at odd times, day and night. And be willing to talk about sensitive subjects without overreacting. When you overreact to what your kids share, they tend to clam up and not tell you anything significant as they grow.

Ask good questions, the open-ended kind. Closed questions can be answered with a "yes" or "no" and close the door on conversation. Open-ended questions encourage thinking and communication, and they don't have a right or wrong answer. For example, instead of "How was school today?" (to which your child may reply "fine" or "okay") try "What was your favorite part of the day?" or "What was the worst thing that happened today—or the best?" Or have some fun with creative questions, like "What would it be like to have wings instead of arms? What things could you do that you can't do now?"

> The patience and the humility of the face she loved so
> well was a better lesson to Jo than the wisest lecture, the
> sharpest reproof.
>
> LOUISA MAY ALCOTT, *LITTLE WOMEN*

Practice active listening. Active listening doesn't judge everything that comes out of your kids' mouths with "You shouldn't feel like that." Instead of responding, "I don't know why you're feeling so angry about not getting chosen for the team at recess," you could say, "It sounds like you're mad and hurt about not being picked for the team. I can sure understand that!" And let them know they're really heard before offering solutions for a problem.

> *Everyone should be quick to listen, slow to speak and slow to become angry.*
>
> JAMES 1:19

Pray. When it's a problematic situation or conflict your son or daughter is talking about, silently pray while listening. Ask God to put His thoughts in your mind and show you how to respond.

A counselor told me once that for many kids, the world can seem like a scary landscape. That's where parents should come in, to help moderate the normal, predictable fears and aches of childhood and adolescence. Sharing time, talking, and having someone listen are often the very best medicine for the struggles of growing up.

And there's a side benefit of good communication: It fosters children's learning and achievement. Research shows that students who do well on mental tests and schoolwork tend to come from homes where there is lots of open communication. When children and parents are talking and listening to each other, when kids feel safe to share ideas and feelings, intellectual growth is stimulated, and those children grow to be more curious, motivated, and enthusiastic about learning.

QUESTION FOR REFLECTION

How well were you listened to when you were a child? Are you more of a talker or listener? If you have more than one child, how do you relate to their different communication styles and stages? Which one of the suggestions above could you use to tune in and be a mom who listens?

10

Cultivating Friendships with Moms

We had just moved to Oklahoma City with our three children, the boys both under five years old and three-week-old baby Alison in my arms. It was a few weeks before Christmas. With no family or friends in the area, I busied myself unpacking boxes and trying to decorate the house between feedings, diaper changes, and housework. All three children had just come through a bout with bronchitis, and cabin fever had set in. Cranky and bored, they longed to get out and play with kids in the neighborhood, but we didn't know anyone. They were tired of hearing me read the same books, thinking Christmas would never come and the grandparents would never get there!

As for me, I was feeling isolated and a little blue in the long days and nights my husband was working at the retail store across town. Until 9:00. The last neighborhood we'd lived in, in Tulsa, was made up mostly of older people and working women with not one other stay-at-home mom, so I was way overdue for adult companionship. It was holiday time, but we didn't have any gatherings to go to. I was still trying to find my way to the doctor's office, grocery store, and discount center without getting lost. If there just was someone to call, or if I knew somebody in the neighborhood who had kids, too. I was so lonesome I could cry.

Suddenly, there was a knock at my door. A mother who looked

about my age smiled and held out a handmade invitation to her neighborhood Christmas coffee that Saturday. With two little ones in tow, she said, "Bring your children, too, and cookies or bread. Join us if you have time."

> A true friend is one who knows all about you and likes you anyway.
>
> CHRISTI MARY WARNER

If I had time! I couldn't wait for Saturday. As a newcomer, I found that coffee to be the highlight of my first holiday season in a strange new city. The country-print-covered table was filled with the cookies, coffee rings, and loaves of warm nut bread that each woman had brought. The smell of hot cider laced the room as four other mothers and I sat around the fireplace and talked about our lives, where we came from, and about our kids. That gave us a lot to talk about—among us there were fourteen children!

Through the window I could see the kids bundled up, playing in the backyard. As we chatted, I suggested that we start a neighborhood play group so they—and we moms—could get to know each other better and have some time out of the house during the winter while the kids played. My loneliness gradually began to dissipate as I got to know these new friends, taking stroller rides, going to the park, or having peanut butter sandwich lunches together with our kids. Oh, the joy of friends!

It's hard to love and nurture your children day after day when you're lonely and isolated. We were meant for relationship, not to be Lone Rangers. We function best when we have someone to share the joys, struggles, and burdens of mothering—someone to laugh with about the funny things that our kids do and the mishaps that happen, or to have coffee or go on outings with. A friend can quiet your fears, pray for you, and walk beside you in the journey of motherhood. Even wonderful, close relationships with husbands and children don't eliminate our need for friendships with other women. In fact, when you have kids, you really need friends. And it is often because of those friendships that we are able to give our best selves to those closest to us.

Remember, the best gifts aren't found in a retail store but in the hearts of dear friends. Without support or encouragement, things can seem overwhelming, like in my friend Jan's case. Overnight she became the mother of three children ages eight, twelve, and fourteen when, at age thirty-three, she married their dad, a widower. After the honeymoon, there were all kinds of challenges—cooking, laundry, and dishes for five instead of one, feeling like a stranger in her own home, trying to corral three strong-willed kids who'd been doing their own thing for a while. She felt so alone and often didn't know if she was doing the right thing regarding the children. Finally, she called Sheryl, a friend in the neighborhood. Through their conversations, Jan began to see the heart of matters so she could respond instead of just react. An older mom who'd already raised two teenagers also encouraged her along and gave her advice when needed.

Maybe, like me or like Jan, you've had some lonely times as a mom. Perhaps you've moved or your neighborhood doesn't have a lot of moms your age. Or maybe your life has gotten so busy with tasks, responsibilities, and hauling kids around that you haven't had time for friendship with other women. You don't have to feel like an island in a sea of never-ending work, toys to pick up, and meals to create. There are moms out there who need friends as much as you do. Here's how to find them:

Start or join a group. There are MOPS groups that are especially for mothers of preschoolers, MOB Society groups (Mothers of Boys), and Moms in Prayer (groups around the nation and world that gather to pray for their children who attend a particular school). Google moms' groups in your area and you'll be excited about the prospects.

Gather a few friends and start a walking or jogging group. That's something you can do with your children if they're in strollers or backpacks. I admire this generation of mothers who are much better at connecting with friends than other generations that preceded them.

Start a Girls' Night Out. Molly, Bethany, and Brook are three young mothers who were busy caring for their kids and got very few breaks. So they decided to plan a monthly Girls' Night Out. On the designated night, their husbands care for the children, and the women go to a restaurant for dinner or have coffee at Barnes & Noble. Sometimes, they do stamping, scrapbooking, or take in a movie. After a few hours away, they come back home refreshed and ready to tackle the next day's challenges. It doesn't take a big group for a fun evening. Even if you have one other mom, you can start a Girls' Night Out and perhaps find other friends along the way who'd like to join you.

Get involved at your child's school. If your children are school age, a great way to meet other moms is to join the PTA or other parents' association and find a way to use your skills and talents to contribute. Working together with other mothers, you'll discover women with interests similar to yours. As you organize projects, carnivals, or events, you'll be working toward a common goal, which will also help develop friendships. And getting to know the mothers of your children's classmates is a great benefit, especially as your children grow into the middle and high school grades.

Two are better than one, because they have a good return for their labor: If either of them falls down, one can help the other up.
ECCLESIASTES 4:9–10

Have a neighborhood block party. Like Elaine, my neighbor who had the Christmas brunch, you could be the person who helps moms in your neighborhood connect. Have a Christmas block party or a summer ice cream social. Send out computer-generated or handmade invitations that your kids help make, plan to serve simple snacks, and ask others who are willing to bring treats. Your party might just be the answer to somebody's prayer! Making and cultivating friendships is always a two-way street. When you bring encouragement and support to another mom's life, you will be blessed beyond measure in return.

QUESTION FOR REFLECTION
How could you be a better friend today by making a phone call, sending a note of encouragement, or inviting someone to a simple lunch at your home?

11

A Mom's Greatest Gift

It was back-to-school time, which for me always brought back memories of chalk dust (which I was allergic to); freshly waxed classroom floors; the smell of brand-spanking new, never-used books; and the lunchroom on the first pizza day.

I'd been out braving the crowds at the mall with my children purchasing blue jeans, lunch boxes, and school supplies. We'd also searched for the athletic shoe-of-the-moment, too, but were unsuccessful in finding a pair in Chris's size that day. Ads on TV and in magazines try to convince us that kids have got to have the latest computers and educational software to be successful in school and that they must have the latest gear to be successful in sports. So we parents do the best we can to provide them.

The beginning of the school year isn't the only time we find ourselves at the mall or discount store buying things for our kids. There are birthdays and Christmas or special times when we find that darling something at Justice or Super Target for our child.

But the greatest gift we can give our children isn't found in a mall, the school supply aisle, or an online store. We don't have to charge it on plastic. It won't affect our bank account. It won't shrink or clutter the floor after its newness wears off. But it yields the biggest dividend of anything we can invest in.

This gift will outlive our lives. It is a mom's greatest influence and the best thing we can possibly do to bless our children's lives—no matter whether they are babies, toddlers, teens, young adults in college, or somewhere in between: a mother's prayer.

> *Again, truly I tell you that if two of you on earth agree about anything they ask for, it will be done for them by my Father in heaven. For where two or three gather in my name, there am I with them.*
>
> MATTHEW 18:19–20

If we let prayer be at the foundation or center of our mothering, it will be such a blessing. Look with me at what prayer can do in the life of a mother:

Through prayer comes wisdom. According to James 1, if you ask God for wisdom, He will never to turn you away but will always supply the wisdom you need for every situation if you will but ask.

And if you call to God first, as Jeremiah 33:3 says, instead of asking everyone else for their opinions, the Lord will show you things you truly need to know but would never discover without His revealing them. When you have problems, He will show you what is your part (and the dad's part if he is involved), what is your child's part, and what is God's part. That way, you won't try to do everyone else's part. You won't be running around trying to be the Holy Spirit and, thus, get in the Lord's way or overfunction so they can underfunction! If you pray for your children and give God your worries, your energy and joy won't be sapped by anxiety. And if your marriage is centered on prayer, there will be more intimacy and strength in your relationship.

Prayer is the greatest influence on the hearts of your children and their spiritual growth. You can take your kids to church, get them the best education, and be consistent about your family devotions, but you can't control or change their hearts. You can't make them love God and resist the downward slide of the culture around them.

Only God through the power of His Spirit can. But as you pray, His heart-changing power works and strengthens your children spiritually. Not necessarily on our timetable, but on His faithful timetable. Don't underestimate the power of mothers' prayers.

Watchman Nee, a Christian teacher in China born in 1903, described a prayer as the tracks that a high speed train runs on. God's power is the mightiest force in the universe, but cannot get to us and those we love without the "tracks" of prayer.

Satan trembles when he sees the weakest mother on her knees, for he knows he has no power against our prayers.

UNKNOWN

Prayer is the greatest resource God has given to make a difference in our world, homes, neighborhoods, and schools—and especially our kids' lives. It is also our greatest tool to fight evil and dissolve the enemy's schemes. When one small group of Tennessee moms met in a Moms in Prayer group every week for one hour to pray for the high school their kids attended, change began to happen. First, cheating, drug and alcohol use, and other problems were brought to light. An honor and dress code were put in place. When the moms began praying that God would either convert or remove any teachers who were a wrong influence, twenty teachers left the first summer and fourteen the next—without a word of complaint from the parents to the administration.

Eventually, several hundred teens were meeting before school for Bible study or praise and worship, and circles of kids were seen praying outside during breaks and at lunchtime. Can prayer make a difference? As 2 Corinthians 10:4 says, "The weapons we fight with are not the weapons of the world. On the contrary, they have divine power to demolish strongholds."

Whatever age your children are, let me encourage you to pray for them. Don't let the crush of activities and tasks distract you from the most important influence you can have on their lives. It's never too early or late to start! Here are some ways to jumpstart your prayer life, in the midst of your busy life:

Walk, drive, and live praying. Ask yourself: What would be your heart's desire for God to do if you could speak to Him about your children? (You can!) What is your greatest concern for them? Write it on a card and pray as you walk or drive this week. You can also pray as you go through your day. Let visual cues be reminders. For example, when you pick up your kids' shoes, pray for their feet to stay on God's path, and when you prepare meals for the family, pray for God's Word to be their Bread of Life.

> By prayer you can live in God's presence with as little effort as you live on the very air you are now breathing.
>
> MADAME GUYON

Let scripture shape your prayers for your children. When you pray God's Word for your children—for example, "Lord, I ask that Meghan will trust in You with all her heart and not lean on her own understanding (Proverbs 3:5–6)"—your prayers bear fruit because you're asking in agreement with God's stated will. And as a side benefit, you are filled with confidence and faith. The Bible is full of prayers to pray for your kids.

Join with other moms. God hears your prayers while you're rocking a feverish baby at midnight, while you're cooking or carpooling, or when you're on your knees—and those prayers make a difference. But the power multiplies when you join with other moms! One way to pray intentionally and faithfully one hour a week is with a Moms In Prayer group. You can visit momsinprayer .org for more information and to find or start a group in your community.

Your prayers are the greatest gift you can give your children— one that keeps on giving far beyond school days.

QUESTION FOR REFLECTION

Who prayed for you when you were growing up? Your mom, your grandma, another family member, a Sunday school teacher? Take a few moments to thank God for them and the impact of their prayers on your life.

12

Great Expectations

The eleven-year-old stepped up to the podium and took the microphone, beaming a huge smile as he began to deliver a dynamic keynote message to 8,000 car wash owners at their national convention in Las Vegas. His parents and friends watched and clapped, full of joy at all he had achieved.

It would be an accomplishment for any child to speak to an audience of thousands of adults and keep his cool, but especially for this boy. Brian was born with Williams Syndrome, which causes heart problems, developmental delays, and learning disabilities. He had other disabilities and medical challenges as well.

Although his teachers said he'd never learn to read and had written him off academically, his mom and dad continued to have high hopes for him. They encouraged Brian to build on his interest in car washes, which ultimately led to his learning to read. His mother, Valerie, made flash cards out of car wash words, and his vocabulary grew and grew. With perseverance and much prayer, their great expectations paid off. Brian became an avid reader and the car wash industry's number-one fan. He was invited to speak at many conventions for the car wash industry and has a dream of owning his own car wash business someday.

Just like Brian, kids who overcome obstacles and succeed have something in common: a parent who has high expectations for them and believes in them, someone who encourages them to keep on trying and shows them ways to use their God-given strengths to compensate for their weaknesses. And they are quite likely to live up to or grow into what we believe of them.

Yet with all the negative labels the educational system sticks on students these days, we often lower our expectations of what they can accomplish. And that produces a downward spiral. The negative label leads to low expectations, which lead to less effort and, thus, less learning and achievement. What we expect from kids is usually what we get!

Kids Who Overcame Great Odds

- She was hearing impaired but became an accomplished ballerina and Miss America. (Heather Whitestone)
- His teachers called him "addled," and he dropped out after only six months of formal schooling. But his mom believed in him and tutored him. When he grew up, he patented 1,093 inventions, including the light bulb, motion pictures, and the phonograph. (Thomas Edison)
- Illness destroyed her sight and hearing before age two, but she graduated from college, was an accomplished speaker and author, and spent her life helping the blind and deaf. (Helen Keller)
- He had a 95 percent hearing loss yet became a top-notch student and gifted athlete who made it as a pro baseball player. (Curtis Pride)

No matter what your children's abilities or challenges may be, your expectations have a powerful impact on their behavior, achievement, and learning. So here are some ways to develop and communicate great yet realistic expectations:

Discover what is good. No matter what their problems, disabilities, or personalities, make a list of each of your children's gifts, abilities, skills, and spiritual gifts. Include strong character qualities and personality strengths. Look for the treasures within each child, and ask God to show you ways to develop these gifts.

Consider your child's age and capabilities so that expectations are reasonable. Otherwise, if they are unattainable—like getting a 100 on every test or winning every soccer game—kids get discouraged.

> *"For I know the plans I have for you," declares the LORD,*
> *"plans to prosper you and not to harm you, plans to give you*
> *hope and a future."*
>
> JEREMIAH 29:11
> (A wonderful verse for your child to memorize)

Take heart if your child is struggling in a certain area. All kids' brains start out immature, and spurts in maturity occur once or twice a year (or more). When a spurt occurs, it's as if a new computer chip has entered the brain. And when that chip starts firing, there's often a growth spurt in learning. Hooray! A math concept that didn't click six months ago begins to make sense, or your child has a new understanding of science he didn't have before.

Last, avoid writing off as failures kids who don't "test smart" and don't make the top grades at school. Also, avoid throwing cold water on their dreams by saying, "You can't do that" when they think of a project or future goal. Hopes and dreams keep us motivated and excited about life. So keep expecting and believing the best, and communicate your high hopes with encouraging words. That's because what makes the difference for a child who has big challenges yet overcomes them is someone who keeps believing in him and doesn't give up on him even if things are rough.

> Children are not things to be molded, but are people to
> be unfolded.
>
> ANONYMOUS

QUESTION FOR REFLECTION

What do you expect from your child in different areas such as homework, reading, and chores? Ask God to give you His expectations for her, and make the commitment to pray, equip, and encourage until the fulfillment comes.

13

Trust Your Heart

The lights in the main room of the church dimmed. We were all in rapt attention as the video began. Along with all the other parents in our congregation, my husband and I had been urged to attend the showing of this parenting video and to read the accompanying book, which presented a system guaranteed to produce well-behaved, obedient, godly children.

As we watched, the formula was clearly spelled out through examples and instructions: If your child doesn't obey you the first time, spank him or her. Strive for unquestioned obedience. Don't allow your kids to say "no" or question your authority or opinions. If they do something wrong, assume it is rebellion or misbehavior and punish swiftly (with corporal punishment, spanking being the most recommended consequence). If you follow this formula consistently, the video promised, the result will be well-trained children with the most ideal behavior.

During the presentation, Bible verses were flashed on the screen, assuring all those watching that this was the biblical way of raising children. Following the video, the pastor of our church boasted that he followed this method and encouraged each family to follow the prescribed parenting practices just as the other church leaders were already doing.

As Holmes and I drove home that night, it was all quiet on

the western front. . .or at least in our car. The program was very convincing, but when we began to talk and pray about what we'd seen, both Holmes and I sensed red flags about this parenting system. The harshness, the rigidity, the ignoring of children's emotional needs were just a few of our concerns.

So although we watched the presentation with the rest of the parents, we didn't embrace its principles. However, seeing it did stir up some good dialogue and help us realize we already had a good balance of love and discipline (and unity as a couple), and we didn't feel that replacing our parenting style to jump on this particular trend would be God's best for our family. We trusted our hearts and how God had been guiding us as parents for a number of years.

It was hard when I was criticized by other moms, like the one who said one afternoon after we'd been together, "You know, you just are too merciful with your children. You err on the side of compassion when you should be tougher like they taught in the video." Actually, I think the Bible recommends mercy over judgment, but at the time, her criticism hurt.

> *Start children off on the way they should go [and in keeping with their individual gift or bent], and even when they are old they will not turn from it.*
>
> PROVERBS 22:6

As we look back over the years and those families who did go with the heavy-handed, forced-compliance method, we saw a high percentage of open and, in some cases, tragic rebellion among their teenagers. Many of these Christian kids grew to resent their parents instead of having healthy relationships with them. And as soon as they could drive, they were out of the house—getting as far away from their parents' values and beliefs as they could.

Holmes and I weren't smarter or better parents, and we made our own share of mistakes. Yet perhaps we saw good fruit borne because we listened to God's guidance for our family, and we parented our children together. It also helped that I'd read some excellent resources on child development and parenting from which I learned that unconditional love is the foundation needed in a child's life, and that children whose emotional tanks have been filled up respond more positively to correction.

> *Fathers [mothers], do not embitter your children, or they will become discouraged.*
>
> COLOSSIANS 3:21

What can you do when everyone seems to be going to a certain parenting class or following the same system or formula for raising the ideal children? Here are a few suggestions:

Don't set your focus on accomplishing short-term, perfect-looking and acting kids at the expense of growing emotionally healthy young people. And don't major on behavior control as the primary way to relate to your child. Meeting your children's emotional needs should be a priority in all your parenting, not controlling them primarily with punishment.[5]

Read, pray, develop your plan, and be united. Jehoshaphat's prayer in 2 Chronicles 20:12, "Lord, I don't know what to do, [for this child, in this particular situation] but my eyes are on you," is always a great prayer for parents. My husband and I have prayed it countless times. I encourage you to do more praying than reacting.

Read the Bible, along with sound resources on child and family development as a foundation for life and parenting. It will help you know what to expect from your children at each age and help you distinguish childish irresponsibility from outright defiance or intentional misbehavior.

Don't just take one resource and latch on to it as a formula. Read widely enough to know what you believe is best for your family. If you have some discipline challenges or are looking for help, you could read books like *Boundaries with Kids* (Cloud and Townsend), *Touchpoints* (Brazelton), and *Parenting with Love and Logic* (Fay and Cline).

Think of a book or resource as providing overall principles and giving you ideas, not as some "Bible" for parenting that you must follow to the letter of the law. For example, if the current healthy sleep book insists that the only good sleep for babies is in their cribs and anything else is "junk sleep," and you follow such a system too rigidly, you may miss out on some wonderful chances to snuggle with your baby in your bed (and no, your baby won't refuse to sleep in his crib forevermore).

Remember, opinions vary widely between experts on many matters of child-rearing: Some say that if you don't give your baby a bottle within the first three to eight weeks when you're breastfeeding, they'll never take one; other camps say don't start the bottle too early because it will cause nipple confusion. Let me encourage you to avoid extremes and not become a slave to any one system.

An easily controlled child is set up for a lot of problems
in life. He doesn't have the strength to say no, so when he

gets to preadolescence, he doesn't have much defense. In effect, by forcing our control on a kid, we are increasing the probability that the jaws of the peer group will rip that kid apart.

KEVIN LEMAN

Most of all, ask for and listen to God's direction for each of your children, and trust your heart as you and your spouse sense unity on parenting issues. And remember, you are the mom God picked out of all the potential mothers in the world to love, nurture, and raise your precious child—and He is well able to give you the grace you need to do that.

Recognize the diverse makeup of each of your kids. As T. D. Jakes, pastor and author said, I raised five children. They all have different personalities. All of them have different issues, different levels of success. That was a learning experience for me."[6]

I encourage you to think about the unique discipline dilemmas you face with each of your children. One discipline doesn't fit all. Which child needs a sensitive, gentle approach? Which child responds to verbal correction? Which one needs firmer discipline? Pray for the discernment to know which is best for each one, and consider the most appropriate discipline for a particular child and behavior problem.

Don't assume that one parenting system is right for all families and all children just because it has a Christian label or the author proclaims his way is God's way.

How wonderful that God promises us His wisdom if we ask for it—wisdom to prepare our kids for life and to be the kind of moms and dads they need in order to become all He created them to be!

Question for Reflection

Think about each of your children. What kind of discipline do they respond to: requests, commands, time out, logical consequences? What does each of them need?

14
Gratitude Is a Memory of the Heart

One day, Heather, one of the moms at the pediatric cancer clinic where I volunteer, said, "Let's start a list of things we're grateful for. We can all brainstorm what we're thankful for. Cheri, you can write it on big pieces of paper on the wall, and the kids can illustrate it. Other children can add to the list when they come to the clinic, and it'll remind us all about things to give thanks for."

Five-year-old Hunter immediately said, "Fast yellow-and-gray cars. That's what I'm thankful for."

"Faith and the strength it gives me," Heather said.

"God," one of the kids called out.

"Heart-shaped balloons. Blood and marrow donors. My purple tennis shoes," said other children.

"Mom!" Cody yelled. "I'm thankful for my mom."

"Volunteers who take time to provide a little sunshine for our kids. For waking up each morning. My child's smile," parents added.

Squishy bugs, double rainbows, puddles to jump in after the rain, the new hair I have growing in, riding the tractor with Daddy. . .the list went on and on.

Gratitude does warm and encourage the soul. In fact, psychologists proclaim the enormous benefits of expressing thanks. These moms whose children were having painful cancer treatments, facing uncertainty and more than their share of troubles, could have focused on the negative and grown more depressed. But as their thankful list grew and grew, it shifted their minds from negative thoughts to more healthy ones, helped put problems in perspective, and gave them hope. The same is true in our lives. And when we express that thanks to God and someone else, it's a double blessing.

Here are some ways to stir up gratitude in your family:

Model a grateful attitude. Give thanks openly for the things your spouse does that you normally take for granted. Your kids will be influenced by your example. Research shows that the biggest impact on kids' values is the relationship they observe between their mom and dad. Also, as you express appreciation for who your children are and the positive things they do, it helps them see how to affirm people (and boosts their sense of self-worth at the same time).

Make a Blessing Basket. Place a basket in the middle of the dinner table and encourage each family member to write their favorite blessings of the day on index cards or sticky notes. Then every few days, read the notes aloud to remind everyone of the many good things that happen in our lives every day (and don't forget to thank God for them, too).

> The most important prayer in the world is just two words long: "Thank you."
>
> MEISTER ECKHART

Play "Alphabet Thanks." When you carpool to school or activities, or when you're around the dinner table, have one child name something she is grateful for that begins with the letter *A*. Move on to *B, C,* and so on through the alphabet as you go around the table.

Start a new tradition. Whenever you shop for birthday or Christmas gifts, pick out small boxes of thank-you notes for your children. Then designate a time for them to sit down and write a short note to each person who gave them a gift. If your kids are too young to write, have them dictate their thank-you notes to you, and let them illustrate the notes with original pictures.

By leaving a trail of gratitude in your family's life, a thankful spirit will warm your hearts, not for just one day in November but throughout the year.

QUESTION FOR REFLECTION

Someone once said, "It's not happiness that brings us gratitude but gratitude that brings us happiness." Think back across the years. Can you remember a teacher, mentor, or relative who positively impacted your life? Perhaps a Sunday school teacher, a pastor, or a music teacher? Have you ever told that person what a difference they made in your life? List a few people who come to mind, then send a note of appreciation to one of them.

15

Create a Quilt of Memories

Alison and I fanned our faces as the un–air conditioned, 1910 train took off through the Green Mountains of Vermont on a hot summer day. We chatted as we ate our brown bag lunches and looked at the beautiful panorama. It was our annual mother-daughter trip, and since we were living in Maine that year, it was a short three-hour drive to catch the vintage train. Money was tight, and we couldn't afford to go anywhere for a weekend, so this overnight outing seemed perfect. After the ride, we went on a nature trail hike; checked in at a small, inexpensive motel; perused a teddy bear museum; and downed a lot of ice cream and lemonade to stay cool in the heat. We were making a memory.

I love the little poem from *Listening to the Littlest* by Ruth Reardon:

> Create a quilt of memories to keep me warm.
> An inner warmth that comes from light of happy times.
> Weave in the threads of holidays, of friends, and families. . .
> Delights of seashore, fields, of city parks.
> The simplest happenings traced out in love,
> Become a pattern, for my quilt of memories.

As moms, we have the wonderful privilege of planting seeds

and building memories in our children's lives. Seeds and memories of caring for them when they're sick or well; sharing their excitement when they bring home awards and good report cards; listening to their side when they get into trouble at school or are going through a difficult, lonely time. Seeds and memories of hugs and hope and forgiveness and happy times together flying kites or riding bikes or reading stories.

Family Memory Makers

- Pajama Day: Slow your family's hectic pace by taking a day just to chill. Declare "Pajama Day" and get out big pillows and sleeping bags. Snuggle, read stories, play games, and watch a movie.
- Family Watercolor Night: Have each person paint his favorite vacation spot or place the family has been to.
- Create a Book: Help your kids make a book about their life. Pick some photos, and have them write about what's happening in each one. (For little ones, you'll need to write as they dictate.) Include the child's birth date, current handprint and footprint, drawings of themselves and the family, and life story. It makes a wonderful keepsake.

Consciously or not, we are always making memories for our children. We can aim for making a quilt of memories that, little by little, creates in our children a sense of belonging, of what it means to be a family, of security and continuity in life. Then when they become parents, they will draw from that reservoir of memories, some tucked away so far they didn't remember they were there, to love and care for their children.

Building memories with our sons was a priority, and with our third child, Alison, partly because she is our only daughter. Also, losing my parents early in life has always reminded me that life is short, and I wanted to make time for just being together.

> What is a family meant to be? Among other things, I personally have always felt it is meant to be a museum of memories—collections of carefully preserved memories and a realization that day-by-day memories are being chosen for our museum. . . . what is done today will be tomorrow's memory.
>
> EDITH SCHAEFFER

I built memories with our sons by throwing a football, shooting a basketball, playing tennis, or riding bikes with them. They always preferred the outdoor stuff. And here are some ways I built our relationship and made memories with Alison, even during her prickly teenage years:

Tuning in. As a mom, I was a fixer by nature who wanted everyone to be happy. I had to work at tuning in to Alison when she said things like "I had a horrible day. I have so much homework I'll never get it done, and the teachers keep piling it on. They make me so mad!" I found that responding, "You must be really frustrated with all that work" instead of "If you just planned your time better, you'd be okay" helped our communication stay open.

Taking mother-daughter trips or outings. Just like the train trip we went on when Alison was eleven, each year we planned some kind of getaway. Another year we traveled to a nearby city for an overnight stay, went ice skating then to a movie, and talked about growing up. Sometimes it was a short, in-town outing like attending the summer musical at the live theater. When she was twelve, I happened to be near Florida on a business trip, so Ali saved her babysitting money for her tickets to Disney World, and I paid for the rest. We stayed with a family we knew and took three days to explore the magical world of Disney together.

> Be a mother. It's a rewarding thing. Mothers and
> Christmas are the two best things in the world. . . . But
> my mother is the best gift I ever got.
>
> MARIE, AGE 9

Seizing serendipity moments. Making memories at Christmas or other special times is wonderful. But some of the best memories are made in those serendipity moments that just happen— like when your daughter comes in after lights out and curls up beside you, or when you take time out from running errands for a smoothie and a chat, or when you take a walk together. In these short, unexpected times dreams and hopes and secrets are shared, things are laughed about, or you get a little glimpse of how God is working.

We weathered her adolescent years, and Alison has children of her own. She and I still love to meet for breakfast or coffee, and we continue to build memories. As grandchildren have come into our family, our quilt of memories is expanding and growing. . .simple happenings traced in love.

What is your favorite memory from your childhood? What's your favorite memory with your daughter or son?

16
Words That Work

This is too hard! I'll never get this project done on time now!" eleven-year-old Katie cried to her mom. Katie had started her science project weeks in advance, but the experiment failed. It was due on Monday, and the sixth grader was flattened with discouragement. Her mom was puzzled by how easily she was giving up. Katie was bright and in the gifted program at school, where she and the other kids were regularly told how smart they were. As time went on, though, Katie put less and less effort into her assignments, and when a challenging task like this one came along, she got frustrated easily.

"I know you're upset, but you'll just need to focus your efforts on finding a new experiment, following the instructions, and doing the work." With only three days left, Katie picked a project that demonstrated the concept of the center of gravity and, with her mom's help, began working on the display. With praise for each part of the work Katherine completed, Karen saw her daughter's efforts grow. She even stuck with what she considered the boring part—writing out the scientific process—and got the whole thing done on time.

Even better, Katherine ended up winning first place. Her mom let her know that it was her effort that had made the difference.

> Too often parents get extremely caught up in the grades, and then they say to their child, "Why doesn't this motivate you?" What is motivating is the whole process of learning and the excitement and challenge of it.
>
> DR. DAVID ELKIND

We all know that encouraging our kids and telling them what a good job they are doing on schoolwork or sports is important, but there's very interesting research showing that we often praise our kids in a way that backfires. Let me explain.

A Columbia University research project studied over 400 fifth graders to discover what worked best with a series of math tests: praising kids for intelligence ("Wow, that's a high score! You are really smart at this.") or effort ("You got ten right. You must have worked really hard to get that high score!").

Guess which kids were boosted in their motivation? Which kind of praise worked better?

The effort-praised kids—not the students praised for being smart—did the best, not only on the first test but also on future tests. Here's how it worked: When children were praised for how much effort they'd put into preparing for the test, they studied more for the next test. When they encountered tough problems, they thought it meant they needed to try harder. As a result, their scores went up, and they were less likely to lie about their marks or cheat.

However, the kids praised for their intelligence began to avoid risks to keep looking smart. In subsequent tests, they showed a drop in effort and interest in the subject and were more apt to lie about their scores or cheat to get a high grade. When they encountered harder problems and didn't do well, they thought, "I'm not good at this," and they stopped trying. Because they gave less effort, these students made lower scores on each subsequent test.

> *Let everything you say be good and helpful, so that your*
> *words will be an encouragement to those who hear them.*
> EPHESIANS 4:29 NLT

What can you do to praise and encourage your kids in a way that helps them and fuels their motivation?

- Let them know that effort and hard work is a key ingredient in all pursuits in life.
- Focus on the work, effort, and time they are putting into schoolwork, sports, or other pursuits.
- Let them know you value the content of what they are learning, not just the grades or report cards.
- Focus on what they are doing well, not what they are lacking. Affirm whatever progress is made, even if it is small!
- When your child brings home a great score, say something like "Terrific! I'm proud of you for working so hard and putting lots of effort into learning the material."
- When your child has trouble with homework, respond with "Let's look at the problem, break it down, and work step by step to figure it out." Refocusing on the task and formulating a strategy encourages effort and steers him away from negative

conclusions like "I'm just not good at math!"

As you use words that work, you'll find the motivational and effort-boosting effects are long-lasting and will help your children face challenges in the future, whether in school, sports, or life.

QUESTION FOR REFLECTION

What is one way your words could encourage your child in a current school subject or learning experience?

A good mother is somebody who doesn't yell at you for getting a bad grade. She understands, because maybe she got a bad one sometime, too.

ROBERTA, AGE 8

17

Connecting with Your Kids

One morning I sat at a local restaurant with our twenty-six-year-old son, Chris, having breakfast to celebrate his upcoming birthday. He was going to be out of town with his wife, Maggie, on his actual birthday, so it was our chance to chat and celebrate at his favorite breakfast place. Chris is our quietest child and, at that time, was a third-year medical student who had a grueling hospital schedule.

Having "special time" is something we started years before when Chris was very young and I realized this sports lover who was growing taller every day wasn't going to sit down to visit, have tea, or shop at the mall with me.

I discovered that the best way to connect with Chris was to get on his turf—in other words, do what he liked and enjoyed. So, many afternoons after school, I asked him when he came in the door, "You want to shoot some hoops?" or "Chris, want to play Ping-Pong or throw the baseball?" and out in the yard we'd go. There, he'd occasionally and slowly begin to open up and tell me what was going on at school or on the basketball team, or he'd talk about a friend, tryouts for the team, or a test coming up. I'd hear what he was thinking and certainly much more than I'd ever have known if I'd just asked him, "How was your day?"

"My twelve-year-old just isn't talking to me anymore. He used to tell me everything, and now he just clams up," a mom told me recently. I shared with her that kids' emotions and thoughts are much like oatmeal. If you heat up a pot of oatmeal, the bubbles come to the surface as it gets hotter. Similarly, as children or teens get "heated up" through activities they enjoy, their emotions and thoughts bubble up to the surface, and they begin to talk about what they're thinking. You begin to connect. You hear what's troubling them and what they're excited about.

So I asked her, "What's your son's favorite activity? What's his 'turf'?" and I suggested that she connect with him there. Her son's "turf" turned out to be golf, so occasionally, she drove the cart for him when he played after school, and even went to the driving range and learned how to hit the golf ball, asking him to give her a few tips. For another kid it might be skateboarding (it would be really hard for me to get on that kind of turf!), kicking the soccer ball, jogging, cooking, or doing crafts. It doesn't have to take long or cost much. Just find out what the turf is and begin doing it together, and the lines of communication will often open up.

Here are two ways to start this relationship-building strategy with your kids:

Be accessible. Accessibility means being easy to approach, being open and warm, not distant. That means being available to give "focused attention," a combination of eye contact, physical contact, and shared activity. As you fill your children's emotional tanks in this way, they'll begin to let you know what they're interested in, what they're feeling, and what's bothering them or making them happy. Most of all, they will feel loved for who they are, not just for what they do, and know you enjoy their company.

Be flexible. Your children's turf will likely change as they grow older. When our daughter was in elementary school, she'd always take me up on a bike ride, but as a teenager, she liked to spend time with me window-shopping at the mall and stopping for a soda. Now she likes to meet at Starbucks for an espresso. When our son Justin was young, getting on his turf meant drawing jet planes or playing LEGOS and, later, tennis with him. But in college, he asked me to meet him at his university campus to hear a lecture on the creation/evolution controversy presented by a brilliant attorney.

> Parents of teens and parents of babies have something in common. They spend a great deal of time trying to get their kids to talk.
>
> Paul Swet

Remember, don't spend time on your child's turf just as a reward for performance or as a duty, but as a way to do something together, as a way to just connect.

A renowned family and child psychologist in our city believed in focused attention so much that if parents came into his office seeking help for a child's behavior problem, he asked them to spend twenty to thirty minutes each day for a month doing something with the child that that child liked and enjoyed, without distraction, giving eye contact and connecting through the activity or game. If the behavior problem remained after a month of consistent "filling of the emotional tank," he offered his counseling services to that family free of charge (instead of $100 an hour). This kind of parent-child time worked so well that when mom and dad really followed through on daily emotional-tank filling, they rarely needed his counseling to "fix" their child!

QUESTION FOR REFLECTION

What is your son or daughter's "turf"? Discover what they most enjoy doing or are most interested in and do it together.

18

You've Been on My Mind

I was racing through the Dallas/Fort Worth airport on the way to my gate when a rack of greeting cards caught my eye. Although I was running late and ten gates away, I decided to stop and buy a card for my husband, Holmes. A Mary Engelbreit design that read "You've been on my mind" seemed perfect.

> In a child's lunch box, a mother's thoughts.
> JAPANESE PROVERB

A few moments later, when I was crammed into the American Airlines shuttle bus with a bunch of other weary travelers, one of the pilots in front of me took his hat off to wipe his brow. (There was lots of brow-wiping because it was about 95 degrees inside the bus.) There, taped inside the pilot's hat, was a full-color photo of his wife and two sons.

The pilot gazed at the picture wistfully, as if he were thinking how much he'd like to be with them right then instead of on his way to another three-day flight schedule. Then he put his hat back on. I don't know how many planes this man had to fly before returning home, but for the rest of the trip, his family would be sitting right on his head. They might be out of sight but not out of mind.

I couldn't help thinking that when this pilot-dad arrives home and his kids and wife see his hat, they must feel loved, knowing he's been thinking about them—they'd been on his mind.

Do your kids and husband know they're on your mind? Life goes so fast for most of us, and it's easy for your loved ones to feel lost in the busyness of your life, your urgent "To Do" list, or your travel schedule.

> Do you love me. Or do you not? You told me once. But I forgot.
>
> ANONYMOUS

Here are some simple ways to let them know they've been on your mind whether you're at home or away:

Plant a picture. Put your family's photo where you'll see it (and they'll be able to sneak a peek sometimes, too), for example, inside the visor of your car if you spend a lot of time driving, or by your computer or workstation. I have a family photo inside my mouse pad, and pictures of my grandchildren are the screen saver on my computer, constantly reminding me of what and who are most important in my life.

Trace a hand. Often our kids don't know we're praying for them. Get some card stock in several different colors and trace your children's hands. Cut out the hands, write a child's name and a verse you're praying for them on each hand, then put the paper hands in your Bible or prayer journal. When the kids ask you what they're for, you can share that you want to be able to put your hand on their handprint when you're praying for them and thinking about them every day.

Therefore encourage one another and build each other up, just as in fact you are doing.

1 THESSALONIANS 5:11

Leave a lunch box love note. When kids or grown-ups find a note in an unexpected place that says, "I love you" or "I'm missing you," it warms the heart and fills their love tank. Greeting cards for no special reason are great, but so are yellow sticky notes on the bathroom mirror that say, "Have a wonderful day. Love, Mom." Even preschoolers who can't read will decode the message in their lunch box by finding somebody to read it to them. (It's also a great motivator for wanting to learn to read.) You can also tuck little notes inside a suitcase packed for camp or a business trip, or on their pillows when you're going to be out for the evening.

QUESTION FOR REFLECTION

When was the last time you told your husband or child you love him in a way that matches his love language? Would he receive your love best if you said it with physical affection, like a hug or sitting close to him during a football game on TV? Is he a word person who likes to read words of admiration in a card? Is he a giver who'd love to receive a thoughtful gift from you?

19

Letting Go

I remember the warm summer afternoon I was sitting in the white wooden porch swing and our fifteen-year-old son, Justin, shirtless and wearing khaki shorts, was sitting next to me. My arm around him, I patted his tanned shoulder as he told me about his plans to rock climb, rappel, and hike at the Young Life camp he was leaving for the next day in Colorado. And then my hand made a startling discovery—his muscles had changed!

Could this be the same arm that once belonged to a skinny little boy? I wondered. His muscles were denser, causing me to take notice of what had escaped me before: My firstborn son was rapidly changing from a boy to a man. He was taller, peach fuzz had become prickles demanding an every-other-day shave, and he was asking for the car keys.

As we rocked back and forth in the swing, I can't honestly say this realization brought a smile of delight to my face. Instead, a tear began to form from somewhere deep inside and made its way down my cheek as I recalled other days of rocking—in the antique yellow rocker we had bought for $10, restored, and stitched a needlepoint cushion for. I remembered how the chair squeaked as I daily grew larger with child and nursed first one, then another, and then our third baby. Memories came flooding back of rocking them to sleep when they were sick or fretful, of rocking and reading *Goodnight Moon* and *Little Visits with God*.

Only a few years later our next son, Christopher, and I sat in the porch swing—on a different deck and in a different season. The leaves on the grapevine above us had fallen to the ground. The paint on the swing had chipped. Our discussion turned to the colleges he wanted to visit before Christmas. I thought how I'd miss hearing his car stereo blare as he pulled into the driveway after school and seeing his long six-foot-three-inch frame stretched out in front of an ESPN sports event in our family room. How will we make it through the week without cheering his volleyball, basketball, and baseball games after school like we'd done for more than a decade?

And then it seemed like we'd only turned around a few times before our youngest child and only daughter, Alison, was walking across the stage in a shiny red cap and gown, face glowing and full of hope. . .and then we were putting her on a plane a year later as she left for a mission trip across the ocean.

I think letting go is perhaps the hardest work of motherhood, and that is why we moms struggle with it. Letting go starts way before your child officially leaves the nest. You may have run into it the first day your daughter picked up her shiny lunch box and got on the huge yellow bus, heading off to school. Or in the emergency room or when she went to summer camp. Or you may have avoided releasing your child until the day your son loaded his stuff into his car, flashed you a grin that cost $5,000 in orthodontist bills, and drove off to college. Letting go happens in stages and also in defining moments. But as moms, all of us face it.

In *Ragman and Other Cries of Faith*, Walter Wangerin says the pain of childbearing is not one and once. It is two-fold, and it comes twice; and I am astonished by the love revealed in such a miracle. First, there's making space in our body for the baby. Then we empty the space at the end of carrying our infant for nine months and deliver her "whole and squalling into existence." But this labor isn't enough. As mothers, we are asked to do it all over again! We sacrifice many things to give our child space to grow, Wangerin says: our schedule, our time, our sleep, perhaps our career, our beauty. But at the same time we experience amazing spurts of joy as we see our child begin to walk, talk, build, and learn.[6]

But then at the child's maturity, comes the "second suffering," when we must birth our child not out of our body, but out of our house and into the world as an independent being. As Wangerin says:

> It doesn't matter how much she has invested in raising him. By stages, now, she labors to let him go. By degrees she loosens the reins, knowing full well the danger to which she sends her child, yet fearing the greater danger of clinging to him forever. And now her hurt is the hurt that he will encounter on his own. (Will he survive in a careless existence, and thrive?) And beside that, her hurt is loneliness. To be, he must first be gone.
>
> This is childbearing at its most laborious.[7]

Since this letting go is inevitable, and our kids will grow up and leave home someday, what can we do to prepare for this time?

Develop rather than control. Instead of trying to control your children from the cradle to beyond college, making them perform and do everything the way you want, think about your role as a nurturer, developer, and coach, one who provides the "roots," or support, for growth, development, and progress but is willing to change with the seasons of each child's life.

Let them know that you are preparing them to leave you. And along the way, provide a loving foundation of values and family guidelines for living, but give choices appropriate for your children's ages. Encourage them to think instead of dictating what they are to think, recognize and develop each child's gifts and uniqueness instead of trying to form them into a version of yourself, and encourage responsibility and independence instead of dependence on you.

Prepare your own heart and life. Find a little space of your own—the sun porch, a comfy chair in your bedroom, or a bench under a tree—and take time out to be still and nourish your own soul. Let God quiet your heart with His love, and thank Him that He is and will always be with you. When you take little breaks, you can recharge spiritually and feel refreshed.

Develop other relationships. Avoid depending on your children for your only friendship and fellowship needs. You need friends! It's also important to cultivate your marriage and not be so totally absorbed in your kids' lives that your husband's needs are ignored. You don't want to wake up when the children are gone and say to your husband, "Who are you?" because you've gotten so out of touch.

Nurture and discover the gifts God has given you. When my children were little, I wrote poems on envelopes and the back of grocery lists. Later, I jotted them in journals, and I attended a freelance writing course at the library and a writers' conference.

Finally, I sent out a few stories to magazines. By the time the kids were in middle and high school, I was writing from my home computer on a part-time and later, full-time basis while they were in school. Whatever gifts the Lord has given you, begin to develop them. Keep a journal. Write down dreams you have for the future and how God may be directing you.

> Kids don't stay with you if you do it right. It's one job where, the better you are, the more surely you won't be needed in the long run.
>
> BARBARA KINGSOLVER

As you pray for your children, release them to God. Cheryl, a mother of three grown sons, learned the wisdom of releasing them daily to the Lord as her boys grew. She prayed often, even when they were little, "Lord, I don't know what it's going to take to conform them to the image of Christ, but I release them into Your hands. Work within them to do Your will and purpose. These are my dreams for them, but I give these to You as well." She was committed to love her sons and bless them, but she recognized it was God who changed and molded their hearts. By releasing her sons in prayer, she stopped wringing her hands and stressing out when one of them took a Uturn. At some time in your children's lives, you must do what this mom did—entrust your precious kids to God. Otherwise, you will smother, cling, try to control, and resist their efforts to become independent. When you put their hands in God's loving hands, you don't abdicate your responsibilities for teaching or nurturing them. You live with a sense that your children aren't really yours but are on loan from God and that you're to care for them but not control them. And you become freer to trust God to work in their lives for their good and His glory.

QUESTION FOR REFLECTION

What aspect of your son's or daughter's life do you need to entrust to God today? What thing or desire that you're attached to needs to be released so you'll feel lighter or more content?

> From the moment we awake until we fall asleep, we
> must commend our loved ones wholly and unreservedly
> to God and leave them in his hands, transforming our
> anxiety then into prayers on their behalf.
> DIETRICH BONHOEFFER

20

Keeping Your Kids Healthy and Fit

My granddaughter Caitlin, four, raced into the kitchen to share one of the treasures she'd found in the backyard while exploring with Poppa. Her little brother, Caleb, nineteen months, toddled in and began going through the things on my lower pantry shelves and tossing them out. In a few minutes, he was out the door and riding his Mini-Big Wheel on the sun porch. And Noah, nine months, crawled right after him at top speed. After keeping all three of them for a few hours, I was reminded why God gives little people to young parents!

Yet while preschoolers like my grandkids move like little Energizer bunnies, they don't stay that way. Each year from fourth grade on, children get less active and less fit, and sadly, many of them (over 30 percent) are obese. By the teen years, 63 percent of kids are sedentary and rarely move their bodies except to get up to grab more pop and chips before spending another hour texting friends or playing video games on a digital device.

What's the cause of this epidemic of childhood obesity? Although there are other factors, lack of exercise and a high-fat, fast-food diet are big parts of the problem.

A recent survey (http://www.iaso/publications/world-map-obesity/map=children) showed that American kids exercise less and down more fries than school-aged children in other countries.

And because of the constant lure of smartphones, social media, video games, and TV, kids just don't move their bodies as much as they used to. Parents hope that their children get plenty of PE at school. But in reality, many schools have eliminated physical education from the school day, and for safety reasons, most children are driven to school instead of riding their bikes or walking.

> For children, play is serious learning. Play is really the work of childhood.
>
> FRED ROGERS

The good news is, your children can grow up healthy and fit, and the benefits are enormous. Here are a few:

- Research shows that physically fit children score higher in several areas of academic achievement. They are better able to focus and concentrate on their tasks and, thus, they enjoy school more.
- Physically fit kids have fewer chronic health problems, higher self-esteem, and are better able to meet the demands of the classroom.
- Exercise increases the body's oxygen supply, stimulates brain power, and even increases creativity!
- Physically fit kids are calmer and less anxious. (See more at: http://www.parentingscience.com/exercise-for-children.html)

Getting fit is just a series of small steps in both eating habits and lifestyle. Here are some things you, as a mom, can do:

Be a role model. Active parents raise active kids! Take the lead and introduce your kids to a variety of physical activities and healthy eating. Remember, kids tend to do as we do, not as we say! We'll look at ways to "move your body" in the next chapter.

Don't leave out P.E. Encourage your child's school to include P.E. as part of every day. Also, talk to the school about opening the gym on weekends and evenings so families can play together even in bad weather. If you're a home-school mom, incorporate exercise like jumping rope, nature walks, going to the park, or shooting baskets into your day.

An hour a day of healthy play! During after-school hours, it's crucial for kids to be active, not parked in front of the TV or computer screen (where the average American child—even preschool age—spends twenty-five to thirty hours a week). After active play, then they can do homework, read, or have quiet time. Avoid after-school programs that warehouse kids with movies and video games, and aim for at least an hour a day of healthy play and several hours of activity on the weekends.

Find out what your kids enjoy and give them opportunities to do it. Not all children are going to be soccer or baseball stars, or even enjoy competitive sports. There's also bowling, kayaking, cycle clubs, running, swimming, dance, rock-climbing, tennis, fencing, skateboarding, and lots more! You could even build a climbing wall on your garage or playroom wall, organize a neighborhood baseball game, or take Zumba lessons with your daughter. On rainy days, turn up the music and dance up a storm together in the living room. Walk the dog and your kids after dinner, and you'll find out lots more about their lives than if you were in front of a sitcom or all focused on your screens.

- Breakfast Sandwich: Toast a frozen waffle. Spread with peanut butter and sliced bananas.
- Fruit Smoothie: Blend fruit, fruit-flavored yogurt, low-fat milk, and ice cubes. (Add protein powder if desired.)
- Funny Face Mini Pizzas: Start with tomato sauce and veggies toasted on English muffins. Let kids use chopped olives to make eyes, zucchini for ears, cheese strips for whiskers, and a few kernels of corn for teeth.
- Adventureland Dip: Mix 2 cups plain yogurt and 2 tablespoons orange or tangerine juice for a terrific dip for raw fruit slices.
- Energy Balls: Mix together ½ cup nonfat dry milk, 1 cup quick oatmeal, ½ cup coconut, ½ cup wheat germ, ½ cup raisins, and ½ cup shelled sunflower seeds. Add ½ cup honey, ½ cup peanut butter, and 1/3 cup sesame seeds. Form into balls.

Make healthy eating fun. Take your child to the grocery store to help choose her favorite fruits and veggies, and to learn to read nutrition labels. Buy fewer high-calorie, processed, low-nutrient junk foods than you did last week. Put five or six lightweight bracelets on your child's right wrist. Every time a fruit or veggie portion is eaten, move one bracelet to the other wrist. Goal: to get all the bracelets over to the other wrist by the end of the day. Encourage your kids to eat healthy to be fit rather than thin.

Let a finicky eater shred or chop veggies and add them to

muffin mixes. Include in each meal a dish you know he'll like, and on birthdays, let each child choose the menu for his "special family dinner." When you focus on healthy food and get the whole family involved in heart-pumping, fun activities, then fitness becomes a family affair—and you'll see the benefits at home, at school, and for a lifetime.

QUESTION FOR REFLECTION

How can you provide opportunities for your children to get an hour a day of healthy play or be more physically active? What is their favorite exercise?

21
Lord, Change Me

When one of our sons was ten years old, we seemed to clash at every turn. I found myself becoming critical of his attitudes and messy room. He was angry that we hadn't gotten him the latest torn-up jeans we thought he didn't need. He scowled at me at the breakfast table and shut the door to his bedroom. He was irritated with my reminders to clean up his room and stop bugging his sister. I wished he would talk to me, and he clammed up. Most of all, I wanted him to know how much I loved him, and yet irritations pushed us further apart.

So I began to pray. (That is truly one of the wonderful things about parenting—it draws us to God time and again.) And the more I prayed for our son, the more I heard God say, "You're the one who needs to change. You need to accept him just as he is. Don't merely tolerate him, but enjoy and appreciate him, preteen quirks and all! There's a time for correction, but this is a time for acceptance."

Over the next few weeks, I prayed, "Lord, change me! Forgive me for being irritable, and help me to be the loving, accepting, and understanding mom my son needs. And help me to see him through Your eyes."

As God gradually answered that prayer, He worked in both of us. I saw anew some wonderful character qualities he had—his steady study habits, hard work, and responsibility at school; the attitude of sportsmanship that made him such a great team player in sports; and what a good friend he was. And even a smile or two passed my way. God's Spirit brought a change of heart in me concerning my critical attitude, and He did some refining in my character during that time.

My son and I played some rounds of table tennis and threw the Frisbee at the park. Even though I had a hard time keeping up with him, my ten-year-old began to share a few of his thoughts with me. I began to understand the things that were bothering him and saw better how to pray for him.

> When you understand third-grade math, you don't belong in third-grade math classes. If we understood what parenthood has to teach us, we wouldn't belong in parenthood. If we understood how to be perfect spouses, we probably wouldn't belong in marriage. . . If we understood our oneness with God we probably wouldn't need churches. Jeremiah envisioned such a day, "When no one shall teach his neighbor saying, 'know ye the Lord,' for they shall know me, from the least of them to the greatest." Meanwhile, thank goodness for the learning.
>
> POLLY BERRIEN BERENDS

While I was with my kids one day, I remembered the saying "Kids need love the most when they are the most unlovable." I thought how that's just the way God treats us. Long before we loved Him, He loved us and gave His life for us. And He wants to mold us and shape us to become more and more like Jesus. And while the Lord uses us as parents to shape and mold our kids' character, He also uses our children to shape and refine us.

QUESTION FOR REFLECTION

What is God teaching you at this stage of your mothering journey? What areas in your life or character need transforming or refining? Thank Him for the learning process and for His patience, even when you seem to go three steps forward and two steps back.

If we don't change, we don't grow. If we don't grow, we are not really living.

GAIL SHEEHY

22

Jump In!

It is easy to sit on the sidelines as an observer-parent, or driver-mom, but distant from the action. Often we find ourselves waiting in the car for the piano or karate lesson to be over or consumed with preparing dinner while our children are tugging at us to go outside. I remember days sitting by the local pool, a bit worn out from the morning's work, watching my children happily frolic in the water while I mulled over the laundry awaiting me at home or worked on bill-paying or some other task I'd brought along.

One summer when we were living in Maine, I'd driven to the beach where I was glad to be able to stretch out in my striped beach chair and read while our kids played and swam. It takes a conscious effort to dive into those cold, 50-degree Maine ocean waves, just as it takes a conscious effort to get involved with your kids in their everyday playtime activities.

That day, I realized it was a golden opportunity to join my kids in something they were having a blast doing. I thought about how in all the hours of going our separate ways in work, school, scouts, or sports, this might be the only chance I'd have that day for close connection in my kids' lives.

"Seize it!" my heart said.

"It's too cold!" my body answered.

But by taking the plunge (after getting used to the freezing water), I made great memories with my kids—memories of jumping the waves, of the sandy peanut-butter-and-jelly sandwiches we ate after our swim, of laughing at the sea gulls that dive-bombed our food, and of the sea shells we collected and brought home in a coffee can.

> Let the children laugh and be glad. O my dear, they haven't long before the world assaults them. Allow them a genuine laughter now. Laugh with them, till tears run down your faces—till a memory of pure delight and precious relationship is established within them, indestructible, personal, and forever.
>
> WALTER WANGERIN

It is in such moments of shared activity that a strong, loving parent-child relationship develops. Along with all the meals, tasks, and happenings of everyday family life, together times form and cement a solid foundation for learning and life. Times of "being there," present and not preoccupied with worries and concerns but really observing, listening, and being involved, convey to a child with your actions, "I love you. You're important enough to warrant my presence and my full attention."

For a while "jumping in" for me meant playing the part of Captain Hook while our granddaughter Caitlin pretended she was Peter Pan, or acting as the troll while she played the parts of the *Three Billy Goats Gruff* stomping across the bridge. She has a great imagination, and mine is getting a little better from her influence. It is throwing a football with Noah, Luke, or Caleb, or running through leaves with them. It's playing makeover with Lucy and Josephine.

Whether it is on Saturday, Sunday afternoon, or in the evenings, look for moments you can "jump in" with your child. Seize these times, and enjoy every minute because life goes so fast.

QUESTION FOR REFLECTION

Where is a place or space you can "jump in" with your child this week?

23

Lord, Give Me Patience

Waiting at the Delta gate in the Colorado Springs airport, I saw a petite, blue-eyed baby girl in a pink-and-yellow gingham bubble suit, matching hat with ruffle, and little pink tennis shoes. When she pulled herself up by a nearby chair, her mother took her hands and, with lots of help and a great display of patience, the baby "walked" through the gate area. Grinning from ear to ear, the little one was so proud. Her feet dragged a little; her gait was unsteady. After all, she was a brand-new walker, at the stage of holding on to things and toddling around but not walking independently yet.

By the smile on her face, you could tell the baby thought she was accomplishing this feat on her own, when all along she was guided by her mother. And when she tired, her tiny hands reached up to Mom, who scooped her up just as she fell. So patient with her daughter's stumbles, this young mother didn't rush her. She gently encouraged her along on her little trek.

"Isn't that just like how God is?" I thought—very much with us, patient with our stumbles and mistakes. Ready to pick us up when we fall or encourage us when we drag our feet along the journey.

Oh, that we would be as patient with our kids as God is with us! Patient with their childish mistakes and failures, waiting when they aren't eating or doing something as fast as the rest of the family, and encouraging them when they are behind their peers in sports or school. And not expecting them to be perfect. Raising children takes lots of patience, and sometimes we moms feel fresh out of it. As Marjorie Holmes wrote, "Oh God, give me patience! With this child who's telling his eager, long-winded story. . .if I cut him off he'll not only be hurt, he may not come to me with something really important next time. Oh God, give me patience! With this baby who's dawdling over his food. . .as I wait for a friend who is late, or for a line that is busy, or for traffic to clear."[8]

> As a mother, I must faithfully, patiently, lovingly, and
> happily do my part—then quietly wait for God to do His.
>   RUTH BELL GRAHAM

Here are some times when your kids especially need your patience:

When they go through transitions. When kids go through changes, they sometimes stumble, struggle, or even regress. The transition from home to school, the change between elementary school and middle school, or a move across town or across the country can all be difficult. You can help your kids through transitions if you are patient and calm, providing support as they learn the new skills required of them, find their footing, and make the adjustments needed to thrive in the new environment. You can be encouraging if the report card at the end of the first grading period isn't what you'd hoped for and avoid demanding that your child do perfectly in everything, understanding that she may do better in some subjects than others.

When they are preschoolers. Sometimes as moms we expect far too much emotional and mental maturity of preschoolers who are larger physically or are verbally precocious. Often we expect younger children's behavior to match that of their older siblings, and we hurry them to be more responsible or achieve more than they're able. It takes a lot of patience to see little kids at the age and stage they really are, not "just like big brother" or little adults, and to rejoice in where they are.

Dr. Louise Bates Ames tells us one of the best things we can do for preschoolers: "Respect individuality. Respect immaturity. Respect your child for what he or she is now, as a preschooler. There may never be a happier time." Read up on the stages of child development, but don't expect your child to develop at the same rate as her siblings or your friends' children. Being aware of the stages children pass through will help you know what is reasonable so "though your hopes and goals will remain infinitely high, you will be able to wait. . .to restrain that impulse to push, shove, suggest, insist, and even punish for poor performance or lack of performance."[9]

Love is patient.

1 CORINTHIANS 13:4

When children are late bloomers. I love the children's book *Leo the Late Bloomer* by Robert Kraus. Leo, the main character in the story, can't do anything right. He can't read or write, he can't draw like the rest of the forest creatures, and he eats sloppily while all his friends eat neatly.

"What's the matter with Leo?" asks his dad.

"Nothing," says his mom. "Leo's just a late bloomer."

"Better late than never," thinks his father.

So every day and night Leo's father watches him for signs of blooming. He watches and waits, but still Leo doesn't bloom. Discouraged, Dad asks, "Are you sure Leo's a bloomer?"

"Patience," Mom answers. "A watched bloomer doesn't bloom." The snow comes and then spring, and Leo's dad is no longer watching as Leo is having a wonderful time playing, exploring, and growing.

"Then one day, in his own time," the author tells us, "Leo bloomed!"

Now Leo can read, write, and draw with a flourish. He even eats neatly, and when he speaks, it isn't just a word—it's a whole sentence that says, "I made it!"

The message of this terrific book is for each of us, as moms and dads, to have patience with late bloomers and all our children, to believe in them, and to know that just like Leo, in their own time and in God's time, they will bloom.

QUESTION FOR REFLECTION

What is an area in which you need to be more patient with one of your kids?

All kids are gifted. Some just open their packages earlier than others.

MICHAEL CARR

24

Why, Mommy, Why?

Noah, our ten-month-old grandson, once pulled out all the packages of chips from the bottom drawer in the kitchen. Then, he discovered the cleaning bottles under the sink, investigated the toy drawers in the next room (which weren't nearly as interesting as what was off-limits in the kitchen), threw all the toys on the floor, and then proceeded to give a quick pull to our big dog Randy's coat. Noah has an inborn obsession for finding out how things work and why, and he goes about it with lots of enthusiasm.

When your child learns to talk, he begins to ask questions, hundreds of them: Why is the rainbow all different colors? Why do we have tears? Where does the snow come from? Why is it cold? Like Noah, young children are driven to figure out what everything is and what makes those things tick. This curious phase can be a challenging time for us as moms having to field endless questions (and put lots of stuff back in drawers and cabinets), but it is an important time for our kids and their developing curiosity.

First of all, let me encourage you to thank the Lord for your kids' questions. Asking questions is a God-given mechanism, hardwired into their smart brains to facilitate their learning, development, and growth. Children are filled with so much wonder and curiosity about everything from roly-poly bugs on the sidewalk to what happens when you smash a banana or break an egg to why they can't fly since birds and airplanes can. So you may be hearing "Why, why, why" all day.

When I was teaching high school, I wished my students would ask "Why?" more, but by junior high or high school age, kids typically don't ask much about anything. A researcher went into high schools to observe students and discovered that teens ask only eleven real questions in a school day besides "When's lunch?" or "What're you doing tonight?" to one of their friends. My students asked a few more than that during a lively discussion, but the fact remains, somehow the wonderful curiosity of childhood gets lost along the way.

> A stranger to our planet, every normal child is born curious.
>
> DOROTHY CORKILLE BRIGGS

At the end of the day you may be at the end of your rope, too tired or busy to give full attention to a whole string of questions. But remember, your response to your children's questions will be either a "Stop" sign (don't ask, touch, try out, or learn) or a "Go" sign (let's think and talk about this question) that encourages learning.

Of course, every time your kids ask you a question, you can't just stop what you're doing and pull out a book or search on your laptop to look up the answer, so here are some other ways to handle your children's questions:

Say, "What a great question!" Then jot down the question on a card if you don't know the answer, and next time you're out doing errands, stop by the library and pick up a book or get the librarian's help to find the answer. It will make an indelible impression on your child to know that you value her questions. I know you can find the answers on the Internet, but for a child, there's something great about being taken seriously enough to make a trip to the library to investigate!

Ask your own questions. If you go to the zoo, query your kids to stir up their thinking, with questions like: Why do you think the elephant has a long trunk? Why is this jaguar's coat spotted? Which one of these monkeys is not like the others?

Encourage creative thinking. Every child is creative in some area—one artistically; another with problem-solving skills; another in music, drama, or electronics. Provide the raw materials of creativity such as an art box or colorful bin with colored paper, markers, cardboard tubes, glitter, pipe cleaners, and so on. Add some dress-up clothes and even garage sale finds to make up a creativity center. Then give space and time for thinking and creating out of the box. You'll be helping your kids become all God meant them to be!

> Children are islands of curiosity surrounded by a sea of question marks.
>
> UNKNOWN

If you remember that there are no stupid questions, only ones that haven't been thought through carefully; if you ask for your children's opinions and celebrate their curiosity; if you don't put them down for off-the-wall answers or opinions, you will go a long way toward keeping their wonder alive and helping them stay excited about learning—not just for the preschool years but into adulthood.

What are some ways you're going to affirm or encourage your children's curiosity and creativity at the stages they are in now? What are they most interested and curious about?

25

Worry Is Like a Rocking Chair

Scrambling out of bed one Sunday morning, I ran to the bathroom for our six-year-old's inhaler. As I headed down the hall to his room and heard him making the familiar wheezing sound, I thought, "Oh no, not another asthma attack. He's supposed to start first grade tomorrow."

> Prayer opens the door to Him who can and will save you from your worries.
>
> CORRIE TEN BOOM

Despite our best efforts the rest of that day with medication, calls to the doctor, prayers, and apple juice, we had to rush Justin to the emergency room at 10:00 p.m. I worried all the way to the hospital. I worried when the doctor said he'd have to be admitted instead of going home after an adrenaline shot. I worried most of all when the next day the doctor told us that something inside his body had to rally—the hospital staff had done everything they could do for him.

I know what it's like to worry about kids, and I'm not alone. Over the years, I've talked and prayed with hundreds of women about their fears and concerns for their children.

With God's help, I've learned some ways to let go of your worries and trust God with your kids—and you can, too:

Children live in the present, and they know when we are with them physically but not mentally. By worrying about the past and future, we lose the present and our children don't have us, even when we're around.

DAVID ELKIND

Hope in God, and put your child's hand in His hand. After hearing the doctor say his hands were tied and he could do nothing more to help our son that September day, I turned to God. In a chapel a few floors below the pediatric ward, I cried out to the Lord, realizing that although I had dedicated baby Justin to God years ago in a church service, I had clung to him through the years and thought if I tried hard enough, I could keep him safe. God called me to entrust Justin totally to His care. As I bowed my head and put our son's hand in God's hand, the fear and worry that had gripped my heart began to melt away.

The best news I, as a young mother, ever heard (next to the fact that Jesus loves me) is that God wants me to cast my cares and burdens upon Him. As 1 Peter 5:7 says, "Cast all your anxiety on him because he cares for you." It means that He not only wants us to entrust our children to His care but that He invites us to give Him what we are most worried and stressed about, knowing that He can handle everything. What a friend we have in Jesus!

I found it helpful to write down the problems or people I was worried about and, one by one, give them to God in prayer. Just like wrapping them in a package, I handed over my biggest concerns at the throne of grace. Sometimes I had to release the problem ten times a day as those worries crept back into my thoughts. But when I let go to the point that I was not thinking about the problem, that was often the point when a creative solution occurred to me or the situation was resolved. And best of all, while I waited for God's answer to come, I had renewed energy to be the mom my kids needed and to enjoy the day we had together instead of worrying.

"Worry is like a rocking chair," a wise elderly friend once told me. "It gives you something to do, but it won't get you very far. That's why Paul advised, "Don't worry about anything; instead pray about everything. Tell God what you need, and thank Him for all He has done" (see Philippians 4:6).

Worry is also a joy-stealer and energy-robber that causes us to overprotect or control our children. When we carry tomorrow's burden with today's strength, it also uses up the strength we need for today—a sure recipe for burnout. I don't know about you, but I need all the strength I can muster just for the next twenty-four hours.

As moms, we have a desire to protect and care for our children that comes with the job description. But sometimes, that caring can turn to clinging and worry. Here are some things I've learned we can do to banish worry:

Call a friend to pray with you. Friendship divides burdens and multiplies hope.

Set your mind on God's promises (such as Isaiah 41:10, 2 Timothy 1:7, Jeremiah 31:3, or Isaiah 40:29) instead of "what ifs?" Absorb the promises, pray them, and believe them.

> Happy is the mother who is too busy to worry in the daytime and too sleepy to worry at night.
>
> ANONYMOUS

Review how faithful God has been in your life. Remember His faithfulness to you in the past and thus far in your life—answered prayers, good things that have come out of difficult times, ways the Lord has intervened or provided. It will start a chain reaction of gratefulness that helps you put your worries in perspective.

QUESTION FOR REFLECTION

What are you most worried about? What is your number one biggest burden or cause of stress? Give those to God as you pray for each concern.

26

Power Struggle

Mom, you're just not fair. It's my hair, and I should be able to do whatever I want with it," my teenage daughter Alison said.

"Ali, when you start paying for your own haircuts, then you can choose the color and style," I replied, driving toward the local beauty shop.

It's amazing how a little thing can cause big conflict. A little thing such as my teenage daughter's hair! It had become a source of a power struggle. She wanted to be creative—to cut off her long, naturally blonde hair and dye it burgundy. I envisioned a horrid red shade that wouldn't wash out, and since I was the mom, I thought I ought to have a little input.

My daughter disagreed.

I tried to win her over with compliments on the way home about how great her hair looked after it was trimmed and blown dry. She continued to think I was old-fashioned. Tension grew between us over the hair issue.

Strangely, tension also grew between the Lord and I. Frustrated, I asked for some help: "Lord, what do You want me to do? You know what she'll look like with hair that color!"

One morning, soon after my prayer, God seemed to give me some insight. But it wasn't what I wanted to hear:

Release her hair.

"What? You mean let her do whatever she wants with her hair? She'll ruin it!" I responded. Now the struggle was between God and me, and only His grace could help me to follow this strange direction.

Finally, one afternoon about a week later when Alison was in the kitchen, I turned to her and said, "Alison, I've decided your hair is yours to do with whatever you want. Your room is, too. We'd prefer you keep it clean, but no more nagging or going in and picking up after you."

With a smile of glee, Ali agreed as she gave me a big hug and skipped up the stairs. While I wasn't thrilled with her messy room or the creative and colorful short hairdos she paraded to the breakfast table, my turning responsibility in this area over to her provided one less opportunity for conflict. I did unknowingly ruffle the feathers of a few of her friends' moms, whose daughters heard about Alison's new-found hair freedom and thought they ought to have the same.

> As a parent you try to maintain a certain amount of control and so you have this tug-of-war. . .you have to learn when to let go, and that's not easy.
>
> ARETHA FRANKLIN

I was encouraged one day soon thereafter when I heard Dr. James Dobson say, "I'm convinced the pulling away of adolescents from their parents is divinely inspired." With relief, I realized Alison's attempts to be more independent were entirely normal. It meant that instead of engaging in a tug-of-war, I needed to let go a little more—and entrust her to her heavenly Father.

When the power struggle abated on the hair issue, she began experimenting a bit. She did dye it a dark brown and a reddish hue, but that only lasted a few weeks. She didn't like it and changed it back to her natural color. She even cut the hair of a few of her friends. Right away, she showed talent, and later, she attended hair design school between her freshman and sophomore years of college which has provided a good side-job through the years.

When conflicts seem to be mounting at your house, consider these things:

Let the line out a little at a time. Think of giving your child independence as similar to fishing with a rod and reel. You let out just a little line at a time. The struggle isn't as fierce, so the line isn't as likely to break. And your child has an opportunity to grow more capable and responsible along the way. Think of how you can "let the line out" for each of your children. List responsibilities you could delegate and a corresponding privilege you could give each of them.

Focus on the "majors" instead of the "minors." You'll temper some of the power struggles. Another way of saying this is: Pick your battles wisely! Instead of nagging and trying to control your child concerning every minor issue you don't agree on, save your steam for the really important things. Sometimes as moms we try to press our own desires in the minor areas, such as how our kids look or the appearance of their bedrooms. We end up wearing ourselves out and causing our kids to tune us out in the process.

For each of us, the majors and minors may be different and will change with the seasons. For example, you might let a younger child choose her own daily school outfits, yet hold to the standard of answering adults respectfully. For a teenager, this might mean giving some leeway in keeping his possessions and room straight, but sticking to the necessity of his being in by curfew as a "major." Think about what areas you can relinquish decision making to your children and what areas or standards are nonnegotiables, then let your kids know these clearly.

QUESTION FOR REFLECTION

In what areas are you experiencing a conflict or power struggle with your child? What may God be wanting to show you or change in you? Ask for His wisdom in knowing how to respond and handle this issue.

I have held many things in my hands, and I have lost them all; but whatever I placed in God's hands, that I still possess.

UNKNOWN

27

Focus on the Doughnut

Our daughter had studied up a storm, putting in a large amount of effort for the social studies test in her new school in Yarmouth, Maine, and was anxiously awaiting the results. When she showed the test to me after school, there were only a few errors, and her grade was eight points up from the last test. But there was not one positive comment from her teacher. Later that week, while I was substituting at the school, I was talking in the hall with him. He told me his rationale for not encouraging his students.

"I never write 'Good work!' on a test or paper or give an A unless they make a perfect 100. Students have to get everything correct to get praise from me," he said with confidence that this must be the right course of action.

Your kids are going to encounter people like this who throw cold water on their enthusiasm or don't affirm them for their efforts. But God has given you, as their mom, the ability to refuel them with doses of encouragement.

One thing I've observed over many years of working with children and teens in school and church settings is that a child who lives in an atmosphere of encouragement has a greater chance of succeeding at whatever challenges or tasks he faces. In contrast, those kids who are unmotivated usually had moms and dads who used negative techniques to try to spur a good performance—

like withholding praise until the child made an A or won the soccer game. They tended to overreact to mistakes and major on criticizing. When we as parents do this, we are inadvertently focusing on the hole (what our children are not doing well, what they're lacking) instead of focusing on the doughnut (what they have accomplished and are doing well). Although these negative responses don't work, parents use them when frustrated or disappointed with their kids' performance.

What works a lot better is to focus on the donut: how much your son tried rather than the score or how hard he played rather than whether his team won or lost. It means highlighting progress ("Hey, you got 78 on your math test this week. That's five points higher than last week's exam!") instead of saying "How could you miss those points again? You knew that material!"

If you overlook rather than concentrate on your children's faults and look for something to commend in their character, academic work, music lessons, or other challenges (even cleaning up their rooms or remembering to take out the trash), you'll find that their attitude and effort will improve. You can also encourage by:

Smiles. This sounds so simple, but smiles mean a lot to kids. A smile is an important sign of approval and caring. Children see themselves in the mirrors of our faces, and what they see reflected there can encourage or discourage.

Hugs. Physical affection fills kids' emotional tanks, so hug them while you have them at home. Countless studies have shown the critical need for babies to be cuddled and held, but the need for physical touch doesn't go away as kids grow. Hugs are needed every day but are especially good for treating problems like bad dreams and disappointments.

Mothering is the art of bringing kids up without putting them down.

UNKNOWN

Snapshots. If you give your child little "snapshots" of what he's becoming and the progress he's making, he'll get some vision about how far he can go. "You figured out my computer glitch and fixed it in record time. That's a valuable talent that every company needs" or "You said you'd feed the dog every day this week and you did—that's what I call responsibility!"

During the course of one day, keep track of how many loving, positive words you speak to your child, like "Terrific job," "You're a joy," or "I knew you could do it," and then increase the number tomorrow.

Don't withhold your encouragement until your kids are older, more accomplished, smarter, less messy, or make all As! This is a simple principle, but it will plant seeds of self-confidence and self-worth in your children's lives. Focus on the doughnut—appreciate and encourage them right where they are!

QUESTION FOR REFLECTION

What is the "doughnut" you could focus on with each child?

Consider the efforts they are making to learn something or improve. Think about their creativity, character qualities, skills or talents, spiritual gifts, etc.

28

Tell Me a Story

Nandy, tell me a story about Mr. Squeeks," said Caitlin, my granddaughter, as we lay on the bed in our guest room. I'd already gotten her a drink of water (twice), she'd gone to the bathroom (again) and wiggled and giggled, and now it was way past 9:00 p.m., when her parents said she had to be asleep.

> Storytelling is an act of devotion. . .that sends children a clear message: I care so much for you that I want to give you the most precious gift I have—my time. During those moments together, nothing but the story matters.
>
> CHARLES SMITH

So with the lights dim, I began to spin a story about her imaginary mouse friend, Mr. Squeeks, going to church with Caitlin and the whole family and then to the park for a picnic. I am not as skilled a storyteller as Aesop, but Caitlin, just like most kids, is forgiving about my lapses in plot, helps me along when I forget a detail, and never tires of hearing a story. Within a few minutes, my energetic preschooler began to relax. And when I looked over as I finished the story, Caitlin was fast asleep.

My friend Kay operated a weekly carpool of first through fourth graders, whose antics almost drove her crazy. One October afternoon, in self-defense and to preserve her sanity, she began telling her riders a made-up story called "The Mysterious Bear." From then on, every Wednesday, her carpool day, the children would ask if she'd tell them the rest of the bear story. They got very quiet, a miracle in itself, and were all ears as she continued the tale of the strange but funny bear. Her son Nick loved the tales so much he asked her to write them down for him, and she did with the agreement that he would write his own original episode.

Storytelling does a lot of great things for almost no cost. It's a way to reestablish communication and a closer bond between kids and parents, as well as relieve stress at the end of the day. You can tell stories in the car on trips or errands, around a campfire, or at family reunions and gatherings. Wherever stories are told, they build a sense of belonging and continuity, especially when you tell family tales about Grandma, Grandpa, and other relatives. Storytelling ignites kids' imaginations, boosts language skills, and most important, offers the sheer fun and delight of a well-told story.

"But I'm not a natural storyteller," you may be thinking. Neither was I.

So here are some suggestions I learned by the seat of my pants to help you get started:

Tell personal anecdotes. Your kids will love hearing about when you or Dad were little—what your most memorable Christmas was, what trouble you got into, what and whom you played with, your first black eye or stitches, your first date, or how you met each other.

Get family members to share a story at holidays when you gather. Looking through old photo albums and asking questions—What was going on in the world when you were a kid? What was life like for you? What songs or movies were popular? Who were your best friends?—will prime the pump of storytelling.

Put your child into the story. For example, my brother George always told his boys "Cowboy Bob" stories, and he'd say, "Cowboy Bob was riding by the ranch and saw Jonathan and Zack. He asked them to go fishing with him and they caught the world's biggest fish!" Kids love being included as one of the characters of the story.

> Sometimes it is the smallest events, the simplest retellings, that touch and change lives. A story that may seem as common as the kitchen sink to me may be the very one that someone else never forgets.
>
> DEENA LEE WILSON

Tell a round-robin story when you travel together. One person begins the tale, the next person adds more action and maybe a new character, and then the storyline passes to the next child or parent. It actually gives the kids' eyes a break from their screens to tell a story from their imaginations.

If you give the gift of storytelling to your children, you may find they become storytellers themselves, passing on the legacy of family history to the next generation.

QUESTION FOR REFLECTION

What's your favorite childhood story—*Cinderella, The Three Bears, Thumbelina,* or a Bible story like "David and Goliath" or "Daniel in the Lions' Den?" Practice the story aloud, then surprise your child by telling it some night when the lights are out.

29

Dinner Time Is Family Time

"Mom, I'll bet I'm the only guy at my high school who still has dinner every night with his parents," Justin complained as we gathered around the table for yet another family meal. "Most of them just pick up fast food after sports and get to go play video games or watch *Friends* on TV, and I have to be here!"

Truly I don't think we were the only parents and kids eating together that night or any other night. But the truth is, because of parents', children's, and teens' hectic schedules, the family that sits down together nightly for dinner and discussion is becoming more and more rare.

When I grew up as the fourth child among six kids, the dinner hour was a gathering place for the whole family and an occasional neighbor, grandparent, or friend. It was a noisy time of lively conversation, clattering dishes, and a frequent glass of spilled milk, usually mine. It wasn't a perfect time. Some nights we kids squabbled or were grumpy. A few nights I managed to hide my portion of squash or boiled okra—which I found extremely yucky—in my shoe so I wouldn't have to eat it. But the dinner table was where I was exposed to what was going on outside my little world of mud pies and paper dolls. There I heard the neighborhood news, a letter from Alaska where our great-uncle was living, what my big sisters had learned in school, and the results of a political election in Dallas, the city where we lived.

The family dinner hour in which a meal and dialogue are shared at the end of the day has the potential of becoming the centerpiece for every family member—youngest to oldest. Granted, it's a challenge to feed babies or toddlers in their high chairs and manage to carry on a coherent conversation, but you can start with a shorter amount of time and lengthen it as they get older.

Although there are lots of places and times you can talk with your kids, a family dinner around the table is one of the best. In fact, studies (including "The Science of a Meaningful Life" Greater Good Science Center, University of California, Berkley, www.greatergood.berkley.edu and "The Importance of Family Dinner IV," a report from the National Center on Addiction and Substance Abuse [CASA], Columbia University) show children who have a regular family dinner time where they talk with their parents keep a closer connection with them, make higher grades, have a lower rate of substance abuse, and achieve more than kids who don't. That's because when students talk about what they're learning, they are able to process, understand, and retain more.

> The shared meal is really what you might call a family sacrament. If you're going to have this sacrament, it means somebody's got to help mother—kids, husband— somebody has to help cook and clean up, and that should enrich meals as sacraments because everybody, not just one person, contributes.
>
> ROBERT BELLAH

Here are some tips to make your family's evening meal a time of enjoyment as well as learning:

Aim for a consistent time, but be flexible. It gives kids a sense of security to know, "We'll all get together at 6:30 and eat." Even if the schedule's interrupted because of an event that comes up, you have a goal to shoot for. As our children got older, we had to plan around Justin's tennis practice, Chris's basketball practice, and Alison's piano or cross-country team training, but we aimed to get together as many nights as possible for dinner. If, for a week or a season, you miss evening meals together, have a tradition of Saturday morning pancakes or Sunday brunch.

Eliminate distractions. So you can tune in to each other, turn off the TV and computer. Put your cell phone and iPads in a basket. The dinner table can be a "no cell phone/texting zone." And although this may sound radical, this short amount of time you have together is worth it to not be interrupted. We are asked to turn off our cell phones in church and in movies—why not during family dinner time?

Offer hospitality to one another without grumbling.
1 PETER 4:9

Encourage your kids to get involved in the discussion. Ask for their opinions, and help even the younger ones feel part of the conversation. The question "What did you learn today?" was a springboard for many interesting discussions at our house. Justin would share about an ethics class debate he participated in on capital punishment. Chris informed us which teams were in the NCAA playoffs. Alison read us a poem she'd written. We talked about school stuff, current events, and activities coming up.

Avoid negative or unpleasant family business like nagging about problems, handing out discipline for prior behavior, or hashing over how many Cs one of your kids got on their report card. You can deal with all those things later, but if you consistently talk about them at dinnertime, kids are going to dread getting together. Steer in a positive direction by asking, "What was the best part of your day?"

Make it special. The meal doesn't have to be a four-course dinner to be special. Ordinary spaghetti can become extraordinary when you pull out a checkered tablecloth and have a themed dinner night—like Italian. Put a tall candle on the table and play music. On busy days you can simplify by having pizza, salad, and fruit slices or by using the slow cooker—one of the greatest inventions for busy moms. The important thing is being together! Inviting a guest transforms an ordinary meal into something special, and making a centerpiece with flowers, a collection of shells, something seasonal like pretty fall leaves, or finds from a nature walk in a basket brings a center for the conversation. Let your kids help you make a centerpiece.

A warm welcome is easier when food is always on hand.

MIMI WILSON

As you gather around the table, thank God together by singing a prayer or letting different members of the family lead the blessing, even if it's short. Make a practice when it's your turn to thank God to thank Him for something specific about each person around the table. Don't forget to share cleanup duties. At family mealtimes you'll be passing on important values, building a sense of belonging, and enjoying each other's company all at the same time.

QUESTION FOR REFLECTION

What might you need to rearrange in your schedule to have an evening meal together several times a week or weekend breakfasts?

30
Building Your Child's Faith

When Corrie ten Boom was five years old, she learned to read. She loved stories, but especially the ones her mother read to her about Jesus. He was a member of their family, and it was just as easy for her to talk to Him as it was to talk to her mother, father, aunts, or siblings. She always knew Jesus was there with them.

Every room in the Dutch house of the ten Booms heard prayers, but especially the dining room. Corrie's father sat each day at the oval dining table with his Bible open and had a very natural conversation with the Lord. "Praying was never an embarrassment for us, whether it was with the family together or when a stranger came in. Father prayed because he had a good Friend to talk over the problems of the day; he prayed because he had a direct connection with his Maker when he had a concern; he prayed because there was so much for which he wanted to thank God."[10]

Corrie attended church every Sunday with her family, but it was her home life that had the most impact on her spiritual foundations, the place where she met Christ and committed her life to Him. It was in a moment of playtime, when five-year-old Corrie was pretending to call on a neighbor while she was playing with her dollhouse. She knocked on a little door, but no one answered.

"Corrie, I know Someone who is standing at your door and

knocking right now," said her mother who was nearby watching her. She explained that Jesus said He is standing at the door of her heart, and if she invited Him, He would come into her heart.

At her mother's invitation, Corrie put her little hand in hers and prayed to receive Christ. Soon after, she began having a deep concern for people who were in darkness and, with her mother's encouragement, prayed for them.

> God asks us to do our part in loving our children unconditionally, teaching them the Word of God, and taking them to church. As a mom, I've had to learn to leave the impossible parts to God—I can't change their hearts or give them right thinking or make them love Jesus. That's the Holy Spirit's part.
>
> FERN NICHOLS

Children, even at early ages, have very open hearts to God and can, just as Corrie did, experience God's presence in ways that leave an indelible and lifelong impression. Many years later, she survived the horrors of a Nazi prison camp where all of her family members were killed. After that, she traveled around the world until her death, sharing the forgiveness and love of Jesus, impacting millions with the gospel.

Sunday school and church are wonderful and needed in our families' lives, but it is we, as moms and dads, who have the primary responsibility to build the foundations of faith in the lives of our kids so they can learn to know, hear, and listen to God. Here are some ways to do that:

Follow Deuteronomy 6. This key passage for parents tells us to talk about God and His truth "when you sit at home and when you walk along the road, when you lie down and when you get up." It means making God the center and heart of your life and teaching your kids in the everyday circumstances of eating together, putting them to bed, driving in the minivan, dealing with quarrels and school problems, and everything else that happens in a family.

> *Jesus said, "Let the little children come to me, and do not hinder them, for the kingdom of heaven belongs to such as these."*
>
> MATTHEW 19:14

Make a Mobile Quiet Time Unit. When you're a mother of small children, you tend to worship God when your kids are asleep, so they never get to see you having special time with God. Then there are those mornings that start with a bang and the children are awake before you, so there's no quiet moments with the Lord at all. Connie, a mom I know, made her own "Mobile Quiet Time Unit" by assembling on a tray or basket her Bible and study book, a calendar to jot down things to do that jumped into her mind and distracted her, a prayer journal, and stationery. Then in the morning, while her baby and preschoolers sat on the floor and played, she'd have a few moments to read her Bible and pray. Eventually, the children started getting their own Bibles and joining her.

Lead your children from wonder to worship. Talk about God when you walk through puddles with your kids after a rain. Point out His goodness in the wonder of a sunset. When you kneel by your children's bed to thank God for food, for Jesus, and for all your blessings, you are leading them to worship. They've got the "wonder" part. Young children are filled with a lot of awe and fascination about things like gerbils, snowflakes, Christmas, and lightning bugs. So we can point them very naturally to the God who made all of this for them to enjoy.

> The walks and talks we have with our two-year-olds in
> red boots have a great deal to do with the values they will
> cherish as adults.
>
> Edith Hunter

Be intentional about sharing God's Word with them. Doing bite-sized teaching, like taking a verse a week to memorize as a family or reading a psalm or a proverb a day at the breakfast table, are ways to hide God's Word in your children's hearts. Sing scripture choruses together. And sometime, just for fun, make tunics out of sheets and act out a Bible passage with your kids to help them get the message. You can even have high-chair devotions with your toddlers as you read to them a verse from a beginners' Bible at lunchtime. God's Word never returns void, and He promises it will accomplish the purpose for which He sent it as we teach it to our children. Then pray like crazy for His Spirit to work in your children's hearts and draw them to know and love Him. Through prayer, you can have the greatest influence of all in your children's lives.

QUESTION FOR REFLECTION

What is one thing you can do so that God will be more the center and heart of your family life?

31
School Choices

Recently, I heard from my friend Cyndi who for months had been praying about and researching the best high school options in the area for her two daughters. After lots of prayerful consideration, she, her husband, and both daughters clearly sensed that God's leading for the year ahead was the public high school near their home.

Another of my friends decided to home school her daughter again this year for ninth grade, but she's also quite involved in the local public high school, where her son will attend his junior year. Her husband is a school board member for their district.

Yet another mom I know educates all six of her kids at home. Another close friend has her children in a Christian school. She substitute teaches there occasionally to keep in touch with what's going on, sensing that this is best for the children.

As I speak to women around the country, one of the most frequent questions I hear is "Where should I send my kids to school: Christian, public, home school? Should we do preschool or wait? How can I know what is best for my kids?" This is a big issue for moms today.

Although I wouldn't try to convince you to put your children in a certain kind of school, I can offer some suggestions for making your own decision:

Seek God. Over and over I've seen that where God guides, He provides. At the school He calls you to, whether it's in a building or in your kitchen, He will provide grace right there. We all want our kids to be safe and happy, to learn and become what the Lord intends them to be. I can't tell you where that is, and neither can anyone else, but I can assure you that if you seek God, if you pray as a family and as parents about the issue, He will show you and light your path. It's a promise. What a great promise Jeremiah 33:3 is: "Call to me and I will answer you and tell you great and unsearchable things you do not know."

Remember, there's no perfect school. Oh, how we wish there were a perfect school where our children would be happy every day and make good grades and love every teacher and have friends that are good influences. But on this side of heaven, I've found, there are no perfect schools. I've looked! Schools are run by imperfect people with usually good intentions, attended by imperfect children with imperfect parents. And each schooling option is going to have its challenges and problems—plus its benefits and blessings.

Granted, public schools have some even larger issues for Christian families: such as mandatory instruction on Islam and teaching on homosexuality in California schools, school violence, or liberal sex education. I don't minimize these, because they are huge issues.

But we can't generalize that "every public school is this or that" because each school is different (so are Christian schools and home schools) and there are so many choices: charter schools; international baccalaureate schools for elementary, middle, and high school; co-op schools. You have to look at each individual school and the character and beliefs of the faculty, administrators, and parents. Don't just depend on a brochure or video about the school. Interview the principal. Talk to teachers and other parents. Sit in on classes as an observer (making an appointment first), and ponder as you watch what's going on: Could my child thrive and learn in this environment? Is this where God wants my child? Wherever you put your children, it is a mission for the whole family. If home schooling is what you are led to, God will give you grace and help you find the support groups and resources that are available.

> Neither public, Christian, nor home schooling is any more or less "spiritual." God calls us to different areas and challenges. And in any situation, He will use problems to conform us to the image of Christ.
>
> DOROTHY BURSHEK

Be involved. Wherever God calls you to put your kids for each year of school, remember you are delegating only part of your children's education. You are still the director of their schooling, an integral part of the process, and you need to be involved.

How? Pray for the teachers, classmates, principals, and your child. Build a relationship with the teachers, go to open houses and conferences, and head off problems by being proactive—like knowing what your kids are being taught. Find something you can do to contribute to the overall quality of the school. No matter where your children attend school, as they grow, you won't believe how important and time-consuming the whole education issue becomes. Sometimes you will even feel that you've gone back to school!

The safest place is the center of God's will.

BETSIE TEN BOOM

Support, don't judge. If someone in your church or neighborhood has chosen a different schooling option for their children, let me encourage you to respect their different callings and the unique path to which God has directed them. Don't judge or condemn the fact that they are in a different place than you are. Support your brothers and sisters in other schools with love, encouragement, and prayers. And please pray for the more than 650,000 Christian teachers who are serving in the public schools every year in the mission field God has called them, some in your own community. When you drive through a school zone, think of it as a "prayer zone," regardless of whether you have children attending there. Pray that every person will know Jesus, that He will bring them from darkness into His marvelous light, that the students and teachers will be safe and protected, and that God will accomplish His purposes as He strengthens the Christians who are serving there.

QUESTION FOR REFLECTION

Have you sensed God's guidance concerning your children's schooling? Are there others you could support or pray for who have chosen a different option for their kids' education?

32

I Had a Mommy Who Read to Me

As my husband and I drove along Highway 281 through Texas one summer, I read a few of the more interesting signs aloud: HOUSES OF DISTINCTION (on top of a Porta-Potty), TEXAS RANGER MUSEUM, and BRAZOS BELL BLUEBONNET FESTIVAL. (Those last two sounded fun, but we didn't have time to stop.) But these signs didn't compare to one we saw in Bangkok, Thailand: SOFT DRINKS INSIDE TOILET.

Highway signs take me back to some of my earliest memories of childhood. Many Sundays, after my father picked us up from church, he'd drive all six of us kids and Mama from Dallas to Aunt Bess's house in Arlington for a big extended family dinner. Sitting in the backseat with my four sisters, packed like sardines, I gazed out the window as mile after mile went by and I tried to decipher the signs along the road. Only five years old, I hadn't been to school yet. My knowledge of the English language was rudimentary, and what I knew of the ABCs came from my big sisters playing school with us "three babies," as we were called. So the signs seemed a great mystery that the "big girls" had already figured out.

All of a sudden, as we passed a small strip shopping center, I saw a sign that I thought said, "Saloon! That's saloon!" I was very proud of myself. But instead of celebrating my verbal breakthrough, my sisters exploded in laughter.

"No, silly, It's salon. A place where ladies have their hair done," they corrected in their big sister way. Even that splash of cold water didn't dampen my thrill over this phonetic awakening.

A burst of joy filled my heart—like fireworks going off. "Salon! Salon!" I read it for myself now, and it clicked. Then I read another sign and another. Mom had read to me the Bible and little books lots of times. But now the world of words began to open before me, and I moved on to Mother Goose stories, Golden Books, Nancy Drew mysteries, and biographies before long. Yet highway and street signs still remained fun reading when I had to be in the car.

> You may have tangible wealth untold;
> Caskets of jewels and coffers of gold.
> Richer than I you can never be—
> I had a mother who read to me.
>
> STRICKLAND GILLILAN

All of us take numerous short jaunts in the car for errands and longer ones for vacations or to go see Grandma. I know you may have a DVD player in the car with lots of movies for your kids to choose from.

But you can also take advantage of those times to play games with highway signs. (Find an *A* in a sign, then a *B*, *C*, and move on through the alphabet.) Keep track of how many different state license tags you can find on cars. And read some signs out loud as you drive to stir up your little prereader's curiosity about the words.

Here are some more ways to encourage your children's reading, even reluctant readers:

Whatever your child is interested in, connect it with reading. Reading is vital to your child's learning—and can be lots of fun if you tap into kids' center of learning excitement, the subject or topic they want to learn about more than anything else. If your child loves sports, get some books on soccer, basketball, or their favorite sport or sports hero. If she is fascinated with whales or clouds and storms, there are great books on those topics. Ballerinas, cowboys, insects, dinosaurs, and dragons—the sky is the limit with the topics available in books.

Take advantage of your local public library. For free you can check out wonderful children's books, educational games, audio books, and lots more. When summer comes, get your kids signed up right away for the reading contest or program. Most towns and cities have summer programs with prizes and other incentives for reading.

Children are made readers on the laps of their parents.
EMILIE BUCHWALD

If you go to the library at least every two weeks and get a big stack of books, you can deposit them in baskets in obvious places, such as by the couch or your child's bed. Don't put the books out of sight, or they'll be out of mind. When our three children were growing up, we would check out at least twenty to twenty-five or more books every two weeks. Let your kids pick out their favorites, but also look for colorful books that push their center of learning excitement and help them get hooked on reading.

Play games that include reading and language. Try games like Boggle, Password, Go to the Head of the Class, Scrabble Junior, and others.

Take your child to a local bookstore to spend her birthday or Christmas money on a book by a favorite author rather than a new electronic toy. Or for a special treat, take her there and say you'll buy any book she chooses.

Install a clip light next to your child's bed, or provide a bedside lamp, and offer interesting books. Then give her a little extra time to read in bed each night before lights out.

Cuddle up with your kids and a book. Reading aloud as a family is one of the best ways to encourage your children's reading and produces priceless memories. Chapter books are especially fun, because kids have to wait till the next night for the next episode. Get one of the Chronicles of Narnia series books by C. S. Lewis, an E. B. White book like *Charlotte's Web*, or *Little House on the Prairie* by Laura Ingalls Wilder, and you'll make some wonderful reading memories together. You can read aloud books that are a bit ahead of their reading level and increase their comprehension and skills.

Every season brings a reason to share reading as a family and boost your child's love of books. Yes, it's challenging today to get kids hooked on books when there are so many digital distractions. But try reading aloud by the fireplace, reading aloud while traveling, or while kids recover from a cold. Make library trips at any time of year. Read recipes together while baking cookies—whatever the time or place, reading is a foundation for life.

QUESTION FOR REFLECTION

What is your child's center of learning excitement? Get books on that topic to spark reading.

33

Christmas Is Coming

One Christmas we were in Maine, two thousand miles away from the family and friends we usually celebrated the holidays with. With no prospect of visitors, and knowing few people in the town where we lived, the whole family was a little blue. One day a week before Christmas, I decided to call the University of Southern Maine's international students office to see if there was a student from another country who had no plans for the holidays.

I explained what I was looking for to the receptionist, a girl with a distinctly Asian accent, and asked, "Would you know of a student who'd like to spend Christmas weekend with an American family?"

"Oh, I do! I will come!" she replied. "I would be in dormitory by myself, for students are going home, and my family is ten thousand miles away in Shanghai." She explained how lonely she was and how excited she'd be to come to our house.

On the Friday before Christmas, we drove into Portland to pick up Zhu Hong. She'd been in America for a semester but hadn't seen the inside of an American home. Having grown up in Communist China, Zhu Hong, excited to celebrate her first Christmas, met us at her dorm with a wide smile.

After ice skating with our kids (a first for her) and helping us make sprinkle cookies, Zhu Hong sat at the table with us for our Christmas Eve meal and then entered right into our family traditions of candle lighting, caroling, opening gifts (including her first Bible), and reading aloud the story of the first Christmas from the book of Luke together.

Rather than being a lonely holiday, it turned out to be one of our happiest. God used that Christmas to cause me to think about what's important. He infused our customs with new meaning as we shared them with a new friend from across the world. No matter what month of the year you are reading this chapter, as fast as time goes, it is not going to be long until Christmas. Since you probably aren't yet in the thick of the holiday bustle, it is an ideal time to think about what really matters in the holiday.

> *I bring you good news that will cause great joy for all the people. Today in the town of David a Savior has been born to you; he is the Messiah, the Lord.*
>
> LUKE 2:10–11

"All I want for Christmas is my two front teeth" goes an old familiar Christmas song. An informal survey of moms and dads shows that what grown-ups want is different—it's two more weeks to prepare for Christmas!

For several years, we lived near a big mall, which gave me a new perspective of how crazy the Christmas frenzy is. The mall was decorated to the hilt, and opportunities abounded to spend money or use the credit card, which financial counselors tell us people usually don't pay off till the next Christmas and beyond.

It is inevitable: Christmas is coming. How are you going to spend it? What really matters? What makes lasting Christmas memories?

College students were surveyed about their holiday memories and what they remembered best. Not one mentioned presents. That may be hard to imagine when your kids want a new gaming system or other toy they saw in an advertisement so desperately they think they can't live without it. But the favorite holiday memories college students rated were: being with grandparents, being with family, decorating the tree, singing carols, and eating a special meal.

In another survey, fifteen thousand kids around the country were asked, "What makes a happy family?" At the top of the list it wasn't designer jeans or the latest electronic device, but doing things together. Doing things together as a family can naturally evolve into traditions and become a way of building continuity and security. Traditions are also part of the glue that holds families together. They create memories that last a lifetime.

> The spirit of Christmas brings memories drifting down like snowflakes.
>
> DOROTHY COLGAN

Here are a few favorite Christmas traditions that are low-stress and inexpensive but yield a high return on warm memories:

Share a Christmas classic. One of the loveliest and easiest traditions is to put your favorite holiday books in a big basket with a festive bow and set it by the Christmas tree or fireplace to be enjoyed by all. Having the basket of Christmas classics close by, you'll be encouraged to sit down and read a story to your children. Our basket started with an old copy of *The Littlest Angel* from my childhood, and each year I added a new Christmas book: *A Cup of Christmas Tea* by Tom Hegg, *Polar Express* by Chris Allsburg, *The Best Christmas Pageant Ever* by Barbara Robinson, and others. New books include: *God Gave Us Christmas*, *Unwrapping the Greatest Gift*, and *The Very First Christmas*. Our kids are grown, but now I'm reading these Christmas books to our grandchildren.

Make a Christmas photo album. Our kids always headed for this album when they came home from college. They still enjoy looking through it and remembering Christmases when they were young. The album is a special place to keep all of your Christmas keepsake photographs, including your photo card you send out each year. We started ours with a few old pictures of my husband and me under our own childhood trees, our first Christmas as newlyweds, the children's first Christmases, their school and church plays, friends and family who joined us for holiday gatherings, our tree-trimming nights, etc.

> The best Christmas gift of all is the presence of a happy
> family all wrapped up with one another. . .in love.
>
> UNKNOWN

No matter how busy we are or how grown up our kids become, we all spend some time perusing the Christmas album each holiday season. It's easy to make: take a standard or large photo album and cover it with a bright holiday fabric. If you're good with a needle or have a friend who is, embroider the word *Christmas* diagonally across the front. Fill with photos, and enjoy year after year!

Keep Christ in Christmas. Look up a few verses on each of the names of Jesus, such as the Light of the World, the Door, the Bread of Life, the Living Water, Savior, Lord, Emmanuel, and read a verse as a family around the dinner table each evening.

Write keepsake letters. Write a special letter of appreciation and love for each of your children. Place the letters in their stockings. Include little reminders of the past year, like how proud you are of the progress your child has made or a character quality you've seen developing. Write the letters on decorative paper with a border and enclose in envelopes. These special letters will become one of the favorite stocking stuffers at your house.

Give intangible gifts, like the gift of an open door or a gift of encouragement. Look around for new folks on the block or in your neighborhood, or find an international student at a local university. Invite them for hot cocoa and cookies or to accompany you to a Christmas play. Give the gift of encouragement by finding someone to compliment or affirm, such as a waiter in a restaurant or a friend who was thoughtful. Finally, take a pocketful of time to offer special Christmas prayers for your children, neighbors, friends, and those you care about. Your prayers will make an eternal difference and be a gift that will last far beyond the holiday season.

If you find yourself in a whirlwind, getting stressed or exhausted, take a few minutes to draw some deep breaths or sip a cup of tea. Reread the Christmas story from Luke 2, and think on the One whose birthday you're about to celebrate. As you do, you'll find yourself refreshed and ready to enjoy the rest of the season.

What are your favorite Christmas memories from childhood or your current family's holidays? What traditions do you want to keep, and which ones should you let go of because they are too stressful?

34

Mentors for Moms

Flo sat at my kitchen table as I served her raspberry tea and slices of homemade banana bread. I wasn't great at baking cookies, but I could whip up a yummy fruit bread or pan of blueberry muffins. We talked about her grandchildren and great-grandchildren, of which she had over thirty; about my children as they circled around us and played; and about the Lord. Whenever I talked to Flo, Jesus always came into the conversation because He was her best friend.

In little windows of time like these, Flo, a widow of seventy-five, and I, a young mother, began to develop a friendship. I didn't know until a few years later that the Lord had spoken to Flo's heart after we first met at a prayer meeting I had visited. He had said, "Flo, I want you to bring Cheri and her young family into your circle of prayer and friendship. I want you to pray for her just like you do your own daughters."

What an incredible gift her prayers and friendship were! She not only prayed for me, my husband, and my children for as long as she was on earth, but she also taught me to go deeper in prayer. Sensing our spiritual hunger, she invited a few of us young mothers to her home to pray with us. Flo had been going into the Lord's presence for over fifty years, so for her, prayer was as natural as breathing. Somehow, she took us on her wings before the throne of grace. And without instruction but in the very act of praying honestly, humbly, and perseveringly, she taught us a great deal.

Flo was also the first person who recognized some potential in a few little poems I'd written and shared with her. "You could be a writer, honey. God could use you to encourage people and give them hope," she said on one of our first afternoons together when I read one of my poems with her. Flo prayed for every book I wrote and each group of people I spoke to, and she was an incredible cheerleader along the way.

And when my teens went through a few rough waters in adolescence, Flo shared so much wisdom. She helped me gain a larger perspective, reminding me again and again to roll all my burdens for them over to the Lord. She prayed my daughter Alison and her fiancé right up to the altar then died peacefully in her sleep the night before their wedding. I watched her reach out to neighborhood kids who didn't know Jesus, pray for the many people God had laid on her heart, and give out of a joy that only comes from loving and abiding in Jesus, even when she could no longer drive because of surgery and old age.

How thankful I am for this precious, godly woman God brought into my life! It was His way of equipping me to be the wife and mother He wanted me to be. As Titus 2:3–5 explains, older women are to mentor young women, showing them how to love their husbands and kids and care for their homes.

My mother was also a great mentor to me as I watched her through the years, caring for her six children, yet reaching out to people in need and exercising her gift of hospitality in our home.

Mama has been gone for many years, but her sayings have brought both a smile and wisdom as they came to mind. For example, her saying "Busy hands are happy hands" encouraged me to keep an art box in the kitchen so the kids could draw while I was cooking. "Cleanliness is next to godliness" is not in the Bible, but Mama lived by it. How, with six kids, she kept the house clean and every stitch of clothing and bedding laundered, folded, and put away before bedtime is beyond me. But I suspect her saying "A place for everything and everything in its place" was part of it.

God has also used other women in my life to informally mentor me. Some of these older mentor moms were in my life for only a season. Like Ray, a ninety-year-old woman in our neighborhood years ago who, though almost totally blind, was interested in other people and kept up with new ideas and current affairs by listening to countless books on tape. Ray was a living demonstration of how to enjoy life and family in the midst of limitations and disappointments. She loved our visits, and so did I. We had wonderful book discussions during the two years I knew her, and she always kept a candy jar out for my children and those neighborhood kids who dropped by.

> Mentoring moments may not be prolonged, but when someone whom you respect says just the right words or gives you the attention when you need it the most, that effect can last a lifetime.
>
> BETTY SOUTHARD

Billie Milburn, my college friend Melina's mom, treated my kids as if they were her grandkids. Though an invalid for most of the years we visited her, Billie offered me a mother's accepting and understanding heart and whispered hope with her gentle words when I most needed it. Our children always looked forward to visiting Billie.

Patty, a dear and zany older friend, remembered my birthday every year, shared her insights, took time to invite me for an occasional lunch or dinner with me, and prayed for me and our family. When I was feeling a bit over the hill as I approached my fiftieth birthday, she told me I was about to enter my prime, the best years of a woman's life she called the "Fabulous 50s." And you know what? Patty was right!

> Many of those who have gone before us—our moms,
> mothers-in-law, and others—are master teachers. If we
> are not learning from what they have to offer, we are
> missing out on one of the greatest resources available
> to us, especially for those of us who are just embarking
> upon this journey of motherhood.
>
> LESLIE PARROTT

How good of God to give me these spiritual moms who mentored me as a mother and wife—especially since my own mother died at age fifty-nine. I've found that the Lord in His goodness doesn't have spiritual moms in the body of Christ just for me, but for you as well—women who can encourage, nurture, and help you learn and grow on your journey of mothering.

Mentor moms also. . .
- help us gain a bigger picture of family, children, and life;
- ease our fears and encourage us to trust in the faithfulness and love of God when things look dark; and

- help us appreciate the season we and our children are in.

How can you find these women? Mentoring programs in churches are great and can help you find an older mom to build a relationship with. But in my experience, it can also happen without a structure or formal program as you keep your eyes open and ask God to lead you across the path of a potential mentor. Here are some ways to start: Look around you in your church, neighborhood, and circle of acquaintances. Don't leave out your mother, mother-in-law, or grandma, who may have a wealth of things to share with you.

Is there an older woman you feel drawn to or would like to get to know? Invite her over for tea or lunch, or ask if you could meet for coffee some day. Let her know you'd like to get to know her, then see what the response is. Most older moms are thrilled when someone initiates spending time together. Whatever age you are, there's an older woman who is five or ten years or more down the road who can hold out a light—and perhaps would welcome a friendship.

If your mom has died or you live hundreds of miles away from her, ask God to show you the spiritual mothers in the body of Christ He has prepared for you to be a blessing to, and who would be willing to come alongside you.

Be teachable. If they don't think they know it all, younger mothers can greatly benefit from the wisdom of veteran moms. Open your heart and ask older women for advice on a puzzling parenting or relationship issue you're facing, tell them something you admire about them, or ask for them to pray for you.

As you cultivate a relationship with an older woman, you will find that your life—and hers—will be tremendously enriched, and you will gain insights that can help you become an even better mom.

QUESTION FOR REFLECTION

Is there a particular issue you have insight into that you could pass along to another mom? Or is there an issue about which you'd love to have the perspective of an older mother? Take the initiative to encourage a mom younger than yourself, and pray for God to bring a wise older woman along your path.

35

No Perfect Parents

When Karen's son was three years old, she and her husband, Jim, got the chance to fly to Singapore to visit her sister, who was living there. It was a fascinating time to be there, because it was only weeks after the American teenager was arrested and caned by the authorities as punishment for having been caught stealing. The uproar from America over this brutal Asian practice was just settling down when they arrived.

Jim and Karen were more concerned, however, about the trip and their son Christopher than they were about this international event. But what an angel he was on the plane ride over—he exceeded all his parents' expectations for good behavior! Since it was a night flight, he slept most of the time, and when he was awake, he played and giggled. As first-time parents, they were so proud of their little boy. They had heard stories of how difficult it is for some small children to travel and were extremely thrilled that their boy was so well behaved. They were even patting themselves on the back for overseeing such a smooth trip.

The two weeks in Singapore, Thailand, and Indonesia were a fantasy for the family. They rode elephants, boats, rickshaws, and bicycles, and Christopher joined in almost everywhere.

By the time the three of them got back to the Singapore airport, Karen and Jim were commenting on how easy it was to travel with their wonder boy! It had been an incredible experience for all of them and, in fact, Jim and Karen were feeling pretty good about themselves as mommy and daddy.

After the family arrived at the airport and checked in, they soon joined a large group of American senior citizens who were on the same plane, also returning from an exciting Asian trip. The elder travelers were in great spirits from their trip as well, but seemingly hungry to talk to a young American family. These lovely, older people poured all their attention on the little boy as everyone waited for the plane. He was in an exceptionally good mood and was eating up all the attention.

With a warm audience, the three-year-old talked, jumped, made faces, and smiled. The whole group had truly bonded by the time they boarded the plane. Christopher got hugs, pats on the head, and kind words as each member of the group passed him. And Jim and Karen got more compliments than they ever could have imagined about how good, cute, and well behaved their little boy was!

Then reality hit. Jim and Karen were on the plane for only a few minutes when suddenly, their angelic child had had enough. Right after the plane took off and the flight attendants were passing out hot washcloths to prepare the passengers for the long trip, Christopher had an all-out temper tantrum.

He wanted to have a tray table to play with, but his row of seats didn't have them. This became the most important thing in the world for him, and instantly, the dam broke. He screamed and loudly demanded his own tray table.

Accept me—for what I am not what I could have been
or even will be.
Accept me—so I need not twist myself to fit your
pattern. . .
But resting in acceptance, can grow.

RUTH REARDON

Immediately, people started looking over at the Covells
and their "out of control" boy. Some of the elderly people made
comments about their loud, badly behaved child. As Karen heard
statements like "I hope he doesn't do that the whole way back" and
"I wish his parents could control him a little better," she began
feeling quite embarrassed and ashamed as the mother of the
troublemaker.

In a full plane, it was impossible to get Christopher what he
wanted, and Karen panicked as she tried to settle down this angel-
turned-demon of a little boy. Both parents tried to distract him,
hold him, and finally clamp down on him as he cried and yelled.
But they missed one arm. Just then, the stewardess stopped by their
seats and handed Jim a wet, hot washcloth. Before Karen could
take the washcloth being held out to her, Christopher grabbed
it and threw it as hard as he could front of him. The washcloth
soared over three rows of seats and landed on the head of one of
the senior citizens from the American tour group!

At that moment, one of the other old men sitting on the aisle
two rows up, turned around, amidst the murmuring of unhappy
people, and said almost under his breath, "Now I see why they
cane people here!"

That did it. The family had been betrayed. The world was

against them, and all pride as a parent was zapped out of Karen instantly. She was clearly out of control, she was a failure, and her child was hopeless. The three of them were alone, abandoned by all other supposed friends and supporters, and there was an angry man with a wet head three rows up. All Karen could do was to hang on to Christopher and wait for the storm to pass.

It finally did a few minutes—or was it a few hours—later. They pulled themselves together, apologized to the wet-headed gentlemen in front of them, and tried not to make faces at all the old people around who were still glancing menacingly at them.

Later on into the flight, after that horrible incident, Jim and Christopher were both napping. Karen thought about what a great parent she had prided herself on being just a few hours before. It didn't take long for her to realize that Christopher's fantasy trip wasn't because she was such an incredible mother but because he was having a wonderful time.

Suddenly, Karen understood how easy it was for her to take credit for something that she really had nothing to do with. In fact, she wouldn't know what kind of parent she really was until Christopher was old enough to make his own decisions and live his own life.

Until then, the jury would be out, and she and Jim would have to humbly seek God in everything they did. She saw how little control she had over anything and how much she needed the Lord to keep her on track as she and Jim walked together on the complicated and humbling journey of parenthood. She vowed never again to give herself credit for those glorious moments when their children (now two boys) acted like angels. Karen reflected that while she wanted to stay thankful for the peaceful moments, she also wanted to remember that the little demons sitting on her boys' other shoulder are ready to strike.[11]

Such devastating moments are going to hit most moms at some point in their kids' lives. How can you respond? And how can you avoid the pitfall of perfectionism?

Put away the myth. The perfect parent/perfect child concept is a myth. The only perfect parent was and is God, and things didn't go so well for His kids, Adam and Eve, and the rest of the human race.

If you aim for perfection in your children and your parenting skills, you will be very disappointed when you or they don't meet those expectations. Yet you can depend on God's grace to be the parent your children need, so keep asking Him for His wisdom, and be thankful when your kids' behavior makes you happy.

Avoid the compulsive drive for perfection. When perfectionist parents put pressure on their kids, they tend to become little perfectionists who are excessively driven, become prisoners of their own expectations, and underachieve. Help your child accept that humans make mistakes—lots of them—and let her hear you acknowledge your failures without acting like it's the end of the world. ("Oh, I goofed on that project, but it's okay. I can figure out a different way to make it work" or "I remember one time I made a low grade on a test.")

Cultivate a sense of humor in yourself and your child. As Karen and Jim look back on their humbling airline experience with Christopher, they can chuckle about the whole scene. It is challenging to have a sense of humor in a stressful moment! But humor can help overcome the drive for perfection and relieve stress. It allows us to laugh in a friendly way at our own and our kids' mistakes, and it helps us avoid becoming overly serious about everything that happens.

QUESTION FOR REFLECTION

Are you—or your child—consistently worried and anxious about doing things perfectly? Are you afraid of failure? If so, bring this to God and ask Him to give you both a fresh perspective and reassurance to gain a more realistic view of yourself, your child, and others.

36

If I Had My Life to Live Over

I was struck once by reading what Len LeSourd, second husband of beloved author Catherine Marshall, regretted after her death. They'd accomplished a great deal and published many books together. Catherine had millions of readers around the world and both had very successful careers. Yet after his wife was buried, he was pained by what they hadn't taken enough time for: taking vacations, weekends away from work, or walking in the woods. They were so busy with their writing and publishing careers that they lived from deadline to deadline, dealing with responsibilities and occasional crises, but having little time or energy for anything else. They marked everything on their calendar that needed to be done, but they left out one of the most important things: just to enjoy life and have fun.

When I read Len's description of the workaholic life these two outstanding people had led, it hit home. I can definitely identify with the tendency to overwork and the need to take a break and smell the flowers. It's so easy to be preoccupied with tomorrow's project, the book deadline coming up in one month, or next week's speaking engagement or PTA chili dinner to plan and coordinate until you feel overwhelmed and all your energy is wasted.

It reminds me of what Erma Bombeck said when she was battling cancer: "If I had my life to live over, I would have talked less and listened more. I would have invited friends over to dinner even if the carpet was stained and the sofa faded. I would have eaten the popcorn in the 'good' living room and worried much less about the dirt when someone wanted to light a fire in the fireplace...burned the pink candle sculpted like a rose before it melted in storage. I would have sat on the lawn with my children and not worried about grass stains. Instead of wishing away nine months of pregnancy, I'd have cherished every moment and realized that the wonderment growing inside me was the only chance in life to assist God in a miracle. I would seize every minute...look at it and really see it...live it...and never give it back."[12]

> If there were one thing I could change about family trips in my childhood, it would be that instead of just driving by a mountain or forest and seeing it through the car window, I would have experienced it with hiking, touching, and exploring.
>
> KATHY SVEJKOVSKY, AGE 20

"What would I have done differently in my 20s and 30s if I had known then what I know now?" asked a 40-year-old mom. "I would have laughed more, seen more funny movies...I would have taken more time to note the changing seasons. ('Can you believe it?' an elderly friend asked me one spring day. 'Can you believe that even if I live to be 100, I will see all this amazing burst of the first day of spring only 100 times?') I would have understood sooner how profoundly satisfying the ordinary transitions of daily life can be: the perfect cup of morning coffee or my son shouting down 'Good night!' from his room."

As I was pondering these thoughts, I considered what I'd do differently if I could go back and begin my family again. I think I would start with two words: *slow down*. Also, I'd give more backrubs to my kids after lights out instead of rushing back to the dishes or to grade the pile of English essays that waited. I'd have dealt with some unresolved grief and loss issues from my past sooner so my heart would be lighter. And I, too, would want to laugh and rejoice more instead of being so serious.

> Since our time at home is short, let's make the most of the summer. Then armed with positive memories, we can embrace more fully the world beyond our doorstep. We can dance into a winter of rich reward, rather than shuffle into a season of regret.
>
> BRENDA HUNTER

I don't know what responsibilities you're juggling, what deadlines you're facing, or what you're preoccupied with. But let me encourage you to take these thoughts to heart and...

- Talk with your family about the one thing they don't want to miss doing this summer or spring or fall, and then just do it.
- Find a way to show or tell each member of your family how much you love them. We don't necessarily have tomorrow and tomorrow and tomorrow to say and show our love.
- Say encouraging words to those you meet.
- Invite someone over for dinner even if the carpet has

a stain or the decor in your house isn't just the way
you want it.

- Light some candles.
- And don't forget, before you tuck your kids into bed,
  thank God together for all the moments you've had
  that day.

QUESTION FOR REFLECTION

What would you have done differently in your 20s or 30s (or
in the last five years) if you knew what you know now? What
would you like to do differently today? Talk about it with a friend
and ask her to share.

Epilogue
Keeping Our Focus

As I finished writing this book, I was in a rustic cabin a block from the beach on Galveston Island. I had visions of walking along a pristine stretch of sand and watching the ocean on my breaks from writing. However, the first thing I encountered after arriving was the stinkiest pile of seaweed I have ever seen. Not one pile, but miles of it. A storm had brought the seaweed in the weekend before, and here it lay being heated up by the summer sun, making the odor worse.

At first, all I could see or smell was that stinky seaweed. I shortened my walk so I didn't have to endure it, and I was so frustrated that the beach crews hadn't cleaned it up that I didn't even notice the beautiful things about the day.

The next morning, I went out and there the seaweed was, still lying on the beach as far as I could see.

But this time I chose to focus on something else: the dazzling blue Texas sky; the little toddler with blond ringlets who smiled at me and said, "Hi!" as I passed her; a dad and son making the most elaborate sand castle I'd ever seen, surrounded, of course, with seaweed, which didn't seem to dampen their fun. Fish were jumping in the glittering water. My steps lightened as a cool breeze of thankfulness blew through me. Oh, the seaweed was still there.

It just wasn't commanding my full attention because my focus was somewhere else.

Life is not a beach. But there often is a lot of stinky seaweed in our lives as moms—things we didn't plan on happening like sickness, layoffs, difficult days, and conflict to resolve.

But God wants us to look up and keep our focus on the call and the prize. What is that?

"I press on to take hold of that for which Christ Jesus took hold of me. . . But one thing I do: Forgetting what is behind and straining toward what is ahead, I press on toward the goal to win the prize for which God has called me heavenward in Christ Jesus" (Philippians 3:12–14). . .

And also not miss the beautiful things He puts along the way in each day.

My prayer is that wherever you are on this journey of mothering by heart, you will receive the mercies God has for you that are new every morning. And that you will experience His unfailing love surrounding you and your children.

May your heart be filled with hope and your step be lightened because your gaze is fixed on Him. And as you mother your children, may you love your kids as you lean on God.

And enjoy the ride!

With much love from my heart to yours,
Cheri

A Note about Discussion Groups

At the end of each chapter you'll find a question. These questions can be used for individual reflection as well as group discussion. If you are participating in a small group or moms' group, you may want to read and discuss three chapters a week.

The chapters are short, so even the busiest of moms can manage a chapter a day. Don't feel you have to discuss every question. Some weeks you may get through only one or two. The idea is to slow down and talk about the things that matter to the women in your group—or with your friend at a coffee shop. So whether you're reading this book individually, with another mom, or you're participating in a discussion group, this book can be a good resource.

Notes

1. Leslie Parrott and Mary Beth Lagerborg, *If You Ever Needed Friends, It's Now* (Grand Rapids: Zondervan, 2000), 21.

2. Stella Chess and Alexander Thomas, *Know Your Child* (New York: Jason Aaronson, 1996), 63.

3. John M. Drescher, *Seven Things Children Need* (Scottdale, Pa: Herald Press, 1976), 59.

4. Brenda Hunter, *Home By Choice* (Sisters, Or.: Multnomah Publishers, 2000).

5. Dr. Ross Campbell, *Relational Parenting* (Chicago: Moody Press, 2000), 32.

6. http://www.brainyquote.com/quotes/keywords/different_personalitites.html

7. Walter Wangerin Jr., *Ragman and Other Cries of Faith* (San Francisco: HarperOne, 1984), 128.

8. Marjorie Holmes in *A Treasury of Prayer for Mothers* by Helen Allingham (Tulsa: Honor Books,1996), 62.

9. Louise Bates Ames, *Don't Push Your Preschooler* (New York: Harper and Row, 1980), 203.

10. Corrie ten Boom, *In My Father's House* (Grand Rapids: Revell, 1976), 66.

11. Original story told to Cheri Fuller by Karen Covell, author of *The Day I Met God*, published by Waterbrook Press.

12. Erma Bombeck, "If I had my life to live over," *Robin's Web* (blog). www.robinsweb.com/inspiration/erma.html

About the Author

Cheri Fuller is an internationally published, award-winning author of over forty-five books, including her newest, *Dangerous Prayer: Discovering Your Amazing Story Inside the Eternal Story of God*, *Replacing Worry with Wonder*, *Fresh Encounters with Jesus*, *What a Girl Needs from Her Mom*, and *What A Son Needs from His Mom*. A gifted speaker, she has presented keynotes and seminars throughout the US and other countries, bringing hope and encouragement to live life to the fullest; find joy in a stressful, upside-down world; and build loving connections with family and friends.

She is cofounder and director of the writers' conference Write Well Sell Well hosted in Oklahoma City, Oklahoma. Cheri loves to inspire writers and speak at writers' conferences. Hundreds of her articles on family, prayer, relationships, and children have appeared in *Family Circle*, *Guideposts*, *ParentLife*, *Better Homes and Gardens*, *Faith and Spirit*, as well as numerous other publications, and she has appeared on many radio and TV programs.

Cheri is a former Oklahoma Mother of the Year and serves as executive director of Oklahoma Messages Project, a nonprofit organization that provides life-giving programs for children of incarcerated parents in her state.

She and her husband, Holmes, have three grown children and six grandchildren. To contact her or learn more about her books and speaking, visit www.cherifuller.com.

For information on the mission to kids of incarcerated parents, visit www.oklahomamessagesproject.org, or on the annual writer's conference, log on to www.WriteWellSellWellOKC.com.

Notes

If you enjoyed the inspiration of Cheri Fuller,
here are two more great titles. . .

Dangerous Prayer

Join gifted speaker and award-winning author
Cheri Fuller as she illustrates—from Bible times
to today—what happens when God's people pray
dangerous prayers. Each of the 21 chapters is
rooted in scripture and weaves together a beautiful
tapestry of lives and kingdoms impacted through
the power of prayer.

Paperback / 978-1-63409-115-2 / $14.99

Fresh Encounter with Jesus

In *Fresh Encounters with Jesus*, Cheri Fuller shares
stories of biblical and historical figures, modern be-
lievers, and her own journey of faith. She shows how
God comes to us through the Bible, service, trials,
mountaintop experiences, and even quiet whispers.
Fuller's stories will encourage women to fall in love
with the Lord anew and live life with gratefulness
and trust.

Paperback / 978-1-63058-352-1 / $7.99